Sudoku Astrology

Sudoku Astrology

Creating Happiness and Succeeding
in Love, Sex, and Relationships

Gerry Maguire Thompson

Author of *Feng Shui Astrology for Lovers*

Foreword by Michio Kushi, author of *Nine Star Ki*

STERLING

New York / London
www.sterlingpublishing.com

STERLING and the distinctive Sterling logo are registered trademarks of
Sterling Publishing Co., Inc.

Library of Congress Cataloging-in-Publication Data
Thompson, Gerry.
Sudoku astrology : creating happiness and succeeding in love, sex, and relationships /
by Gerry Maguire Thompson.
p. cm.
Includes index.
ISBN 978-1-4027-5136-3
1. Astrology, Oriental. 2. Sudoku--Miscellanea. I. Title.
BF1714.A75T46 2009
133.5'925--dc22
2008043108

2   4   6   8   10   9   7   5   3   1

Published by Sterling Publishing Co., Inc.
387 Park Avenue South, New York, NY 10016
© 2009 by Gerry Maguire Thompson
Distributed in Canada by Sterling Publishing
c/o Canadian Manda Group, 165 Dufferin Street
Toronto, Ontario, Canada M6K 3H6
Distributed in the United Kingdom by GMC Distribution Services
Castle Place, 166 High Street, Lewes, East Sussex, England BN7 1XU
Distributed in Australia by Capricorn Link (Australia) Pty. Ltd.
P.O. Box 704, Windsor, NSW 2756, Australia

Sterling ISBN 978-1-4027-5136-3

For information about custom editions, special sales, premium and
corporate purchases, please contact Sterling Special Sales
Department at 800-805-5489 or specialsales@sterlingpublishing.com.

"Every situation in life is an opportunity to create value."
—GERRY THOMPSON

"One day of life is more valuable than all the treasures of the universe."
—NICHIREN DAISHONIN

"Everyone has a vast and unsurpassed palace within,
resplendent with infinite treasures of the universe. When we open the door
to that palace, wherever we are, we can find happiness."
—DAISAKU IKEDA

Contents

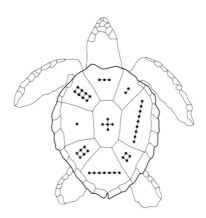

Foreword

I am pleased to introduce this welcome book on a fascinating form of astrology, also known as Nine Star Ki, which I introduced from Japan to the West in the 1970s.

I have known Gerry personally since 1981 when he studied with me in Boston, Massachusetts, and assisted me in macrobiotic consultations. That year Gerry also produced the first major feature on this subject in the West in an international magazine, the influential *East-West Journal.*

Gerry has an admirable ability to explain ancient Oriental concepts, which are subtle, complex, and often arcane, in a simple and highly accessible manner that is ideally suited to the modern reader.

Recovery of the traditional teachings of the past such as these, as well as development of new planetary approaches, are keys to creating a world of enduring health, happiness, and peace.

—*Michio Kushi*

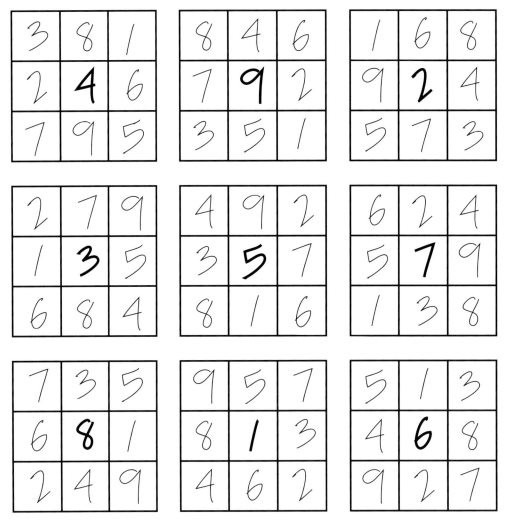

These nine magic squares describe the arrangement of the elemental influences over the nine-year cycle of change (see Chapter 2).

Introduction

You know that sudoku is an addictive and compelling game that's been sweeping the world. But did you know that it derives from a numerological system that's been used for astrology, divination, and life planning for thousands of years?

My wife is totally hooked on sudoku—she loves it. She does sudoku puzzles in the morning before work, after coming home for work, and while getting ready to go out for the evening. She does sudoku in the garden, in the bath, in bed. She does sudoku all the time.

Why is sudoku so addictive? There's no denying that there's something seductive and alluring about those nine numbers and the elegant way they relate to one another in their ever-changing grid. Perhaps we unconsciously sense that there's something of deeper significance in them, but we don't know what it is. This book will explain exactly what that significance is and show you how you can use it to make life a better experience. And you can still be addicted to doing the puzzles!

THE ORIGINS OF THE ORACLE

Sudoku astrology, or the astrology of the magic square, is an extraordinary oracle and divining method of great antiquity, dating back as far as 5000 BCE. It uses exactly the same system as the sudoku game that is all the rage—an arrangement of the numbers 1 to 9 within the squares of a 3 by 3 grid—but it is much more useful and revealing than a mere puzzle. In fact, the magic square is an integral part of the same Oriental cosmology that has given us *I Ching* divination, *tai chi,* and *feng shui,* based on the same understanding of energy patterns over time as they influence the Earth and the affairs of humankind. It has been used into modern times in China, Japan, and other parts of the Orient, but it is only now coming to the attention of the West as a tool for modern living.

Though I use the term astrology (from the Latin *astra,* stars), the influences involved go beyond the stars themselves. While Western zodiac astrology measures the specific influences associated with the celestial bodies and their movements, and the Chinese astrological system of the twelve animals lays emphasis on the influences of the Earth in particular, sudoku astrology reveals the broader interacting energies of heaven and Earth, the cosmic energies shaping the universe. It's the ultimate holistic view of life, rooted in the ancient Chinese concepts of *yin and yang, chi,* and the *Five Elements,* which are the basis of all traditional Oriental disciplines—from aikido to flower arranging and from acupuncture to Zen.

DESTINY VS. UNDERSTANDING

The Chinese are nothing if not pragmatic, and this astrological system evolved as a very practical, down-to-earth business. Although it provides profound and diverse information about people and relationships, it's a lot more simple and straightforward to grasp and put into practice than most other divining systems. This book is all about working with the energies of the universe as they affect *you,* the unique individual—not ignoring them, not working against them, but harmonizing with them and using them constructively. This is the way to make the most of life's opportunities, to maximize effectiveness and happiness. This is what sudoku astrology is all about.

The oracle is remarkably diverse in its scope and applications. It gives you insight into your unique potential for health and well-being, love and romance, mental and emotional development, career orientation and work fulfillment, and also spiritual growth. It gives indications for understanding others and making the best of every relationship. And it gives practical information on which to base any kind of decision making, whether you're taking the long view or the short, by showing which energies are at work in a given year, in a given month, or just for today. Used with understanding, it holds a key to deeper self-knowledge and greater fulfillment for each and every individual. It's a wonderful blending of Oriental cosmology with the timeless fascination of numbers.

The methods in this book won't help you predict what's going to happen; I don't believe that's what sudoku astrology is for. They will help you understand your own complex range of qualities better, so you can make the most of your strengths and work effectively with traits that may be problematic. Instead of hoping to be "lucky"—instead of letting your happiness depend on winning the lottery or meeting someone who will secure your future for you—you can take action to improve your situation and maximize your potential. You can be your true self rather than trying to be someone you're not.

Sudoku astrology, then, is a tool for:

- Understanding yourself better and maximizing your potential
- Understanding what makes other people tick
- Creating successful relationships and partnerships with these other people
- Planning and making important decisions at the most effective time
- Building an appropriate and satisfying career
- Charting a life path that's right for you

WHAT YOU'LL FIND IN THIS BOOK

First we'll take a little time to understand something of how sudoku astrology works, because it's distinctly different from other astrological systems you may have encountered.

(You'll also find it extremely fascinating.) The basics are explained in Chapter 1. Then you'll be ready to start finding out stuff about yourself. Chapter 2 shows what sudoku astrology can tell you about your own personal characteristics and potential.

After that, you'll find it really interesting to apply the same analysis to other people you deal with in life, so as to understand them better. Whether it's the person you've been married to for forty years, or someone you work with, or a close friend or member of your family, you'll discover his or her inner workings in Chapter 3.

Chapter 4 shows how to examine the potential in a relationship with any other person, and how to make the most of this potential. You'll learn to combine astrological information about yourself with information about the other person and interpret the results as practical indicators—and you'll see clear examples of how this works.

Next we'll look at how your astrological potential changes over time. This insight will help you in looking back over the past, looking forward into the future, or choosing auspicious timing for important decisions or steps you may wish to take. If you've had recurring cycles of experience—patterns you'd like to stop repeating—you'll come to understand why, and find out what to do to improve the situation, in Chapter 5.

Chapter 6 provides you with further ideas for putting the principles of sudoku astrology into practice and leaves you with some powerful tools for making the most of your life.

The Principles of the Magic Square

Sudoku is a Japanese term meaning *the numbers must only occur once,* but the concept was not invented in Japan, as many believe. The puzzles so popular today derived from the work of Swiss mathematician Leonhard Euler, who lived from 1707 to 1783. Euler worked with *magic squares,* or squares with nine cells containing the numbers 1 to 9, always arranged so that rows in any direction added up to the same number: 15.

Sudoku puzzles were first published in the late 1970s in the United States. But sudoku is much more than a recreational game. Through the ages, the sudoku system has been used in one form or another by prehistoric shamans, Chinese emperors, Arab mystics, Hebrew cabbalists, and European physicists. And all of these uses have flowed into the development of this very valuable tool for living today—sudoku astrology.

THE ANCIENT ROOTS OF ASTROLOGY

The magic square was probably introduced to Europe via Moorish Spain by the Arabs, who had a deep interest in the mystical properties of numbers, borne out by documents from as early as the ninth century. Prior to this, cabbalists and other mystics in different cultures also attributed esoteric significance to numerology and the magic square.

The concept of the magic square came to the Arabs and these others from China, probably by way of India, which was a great clearinghouse of spiritual ideas from around the year 1000 CE onward. It's when we look back to these roots in China that things really become interesting—and from our point of view today, they also become useful.

In prehistoric China, generations of sages dedicated their lives to studying the workings of cosmic energies in all earthly and heavenly phenomena. Over millennia, they succeeded in cataloging a series of principles or natural laws that governed the operation of these energies. First they identified the influences of complementary *yin* and *yang* forces; then they classified these energies further into the classical system of the *Five Elements*, which in turn were broken down into nine stages of energy transformation through which all changing phenomena pass. It is upon this system of Chinese numerology—the *nine numbers*—that the magic square oracle builds, to produce a comprehensive examination of earthly and celestial influences on the natural world and on human activity. The very earliest written form of these principles that archaeologists have found is in the form of hieroglyphics carved into the cells of a turtle shell, a shamanistic artifact dating all the way back to 5000 BCE.

So when sudoku made its way from the United States to the Orient in the 1980s, things had come full circle. By 1986, sudoku was one of the most popular puzzles in Japan. In 2004, the London *Times* launched its first sudoku issue, and the trend spread like wildfire through European and New World media. In 2005, it arrived back in the United States, via the *New York Post*. Now it's truly worldwide, and all over the place—on TV, on the Internet, and even on your mobile phone.

THE LEGEND OF THE TURTLE

There is a very old Chinese legend that tells how the original concept of sudoku astrology was first discovered. It is set in the time of the very earliest civilization in China, which grew up along the Great Yellow River around 2000 BCE, or 4000 years ago.

1-1. The ancient Chinese oracle of the turtle shell.

The riverside towns and villages were repeatedly wiped out by floods when the river burst its banks over and over for many generations. Then along came a thoughtful and contemplative man by the name of Fu Hsi, who had the idea of constructing earthworks to contain the flooding river. The idea worked, and Fu Hsi became emperor.

While sitting in meditation on the banks of the river one day, Fu Hsi noticed a turtle coming out of the water. In those times, turtles were considered sacred creatures and bearers of omens, so he paid particular attention. According to the story, he noticed an unusual pattern of markings on the turtle's back—a collection of eight hieroglyphics arranged in a circle with a ninth hieroglyph in the center (Figure 1-1). The emperor imprinted this pattern of marks on his mind, and on returning home he engaged the most eminent sages in the land to interpret the oracle. From this beginning, it is said, grew the body of knowledge about the workings of the cosmic energies upon which sudoku astrology—and all of Chinese culture—is founded.

This legend is probably a mythological rendering of the history surrounding the earliest shamanic practices of divination, which were indeed based upon the use of the turtle shell. A question would be ritually put to the shaman, who would then apply heat to the inner surface of one of the turtle shell's indentations. The heat would cause cracks to appear on the outer surface, and the shaman would interpret these as indicators of the omens. Over time, particular patterns of cracks that proved consistently reliable would be permanently inscribed on the outer surface of the shell, which became an oracle that could be consulted in its own right, without the application of heat.

All this, of course, took place in a purely oral tradition before true writing was invented. The earliest written records of astrological prediction for the rulers of those times have also been found on these shell relics. The eight trigrams that evolved from the hieroglyphics of the turtle legend eventually became the basis for the great classic of Oriental wisdom, the *I Ching* or *Book of Changes*. In that book, the trigrams are expanded into a method of interpreting all phenomena, understanding events, and determining the most auspicious actions to take. The classic arrangement of these trigrams—the key to everything in sudoku astrology—is called the *magic square*. The magic square also figures in feng shui, where it is known as the *lo shu* map and is used to discern how the energies in physical spaces will affect people.

You'll notice, of course, that this simple arrangement of nine numerical characters, which evolved from the ancient Chinese trigrams, is the key to the sudoku puzzle format, in which the numbers 1 through 9 each occur exactly once. It's also the basis of a powerful and versatile system of divination, or the interpretation of life's possibilities. Once you've grasped the basics of how the square works, you'll be able to apply it to your life at many levels. First, we'll look more closely at the cosmic forces it describes.

THE ENERGIES OF THE COSMOS

Most spiritual traditions acknowledge the primary importance of the formative forces or energies that activate all life. These life forces are known as *ki* in Japan, *prana* in India, and *chi* or *qi* in China. Astrology, broadly speaking, is the study of the patterns of change in these energies over time. Basically, the magic square is a kind of short-hand formula that summarizes the interaction of these influential energies; using it, we can gain insight into the nature of any phenomenon whatsoever—including, of course, ourselves.

Yin and Yang

Even the earliest peoples developed a sense of the cosmic influences acting on humanity, recognizing a dimension to human existence that goes beyond the mundane. Shamanism, the most ancient of religions, acknowledged the inter-connectedness of all things—including human beings—dominated by the interplay of the two greatest forces of all, the energies of the heavens and the energies of Earth. This view still survives in traditions such as Native American

1-2. The cycle of yin and yang.

cosmology, in which Father Heaven and Mother Earth are seen as the originators of all things. The same worldview existed in ancient China, under a different name: the all-embracing interaction of *yin* and *yang* that similarly generates and characterizes all of life, shown symbolically in Figure 1-2.

In Oriental cosmology, all life on Earth is profoundly affected by these two influences. One is the heavenly yang energy, which is exemplified by the life-giving radiation that showers down toward our planet from the sun, other stars, constellations, and galaxies, and is most obviously embodied in the downward force of gravity. The other is the opposing and balancing yin energy that originates in the central core of the Earth and expands outward, as physically manifested in the upward growth of trees and plants.

These two energy fields mix powerfully in all phenomena, especially at the surface of the Earth, where we live. Nothing is all yin or all yang; the complementary forces are always mingling in a dynamically changing state of opposition and balance. So all forms of life are animated by this subtle interplay of these influences, which changes from year to year, from season to season, and even from moment to moment. This is the basis of the astrology of time.

Modern humanity tends to forget this subtle interconnectedness of all things, and its fundamental significance to our lives. Scientists are beginning to become aware of the web of connection that sudoku astrology defines. "Touch a leaf," modern quantum physicists are telling us, "and you disturb a star."

The Five Elements

The Oriental system of Five Elements, which evolved from the concept of yin and yang, is a simple yet profound method of gaining further insight into the workings of life. The Five-Element system has been used for thousands of years as the basis of every classical Oriental discipline, from medicine to archery to the tea ceremony. It is important to understand it in order to move one step closer to the core of sudoku astrology.

The Five-Element system takes an important step beyond the distinction of yin and yang. First, it recognizes that all living things are in a state of interplay between yin and yang energies, and that this interplay follows predictable repeating patterns: cycles of ascending and descending energies, expansion and contraction, heat and cold, light and dark, day and night, birth and death. It also names and describes the archetypal stages within these cycles, such as the seasons the Earth passes through on the way from winter to summer and on to winter again.

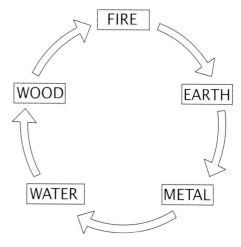

1-3. The cycle of the five elements.

In every transformation of energies from one extreme to another, there are five universal stages, each named for an element and traditionally illustrated by examples from the world of nature. Life moves through these five stages in a continuous cycle, repeating without beginning or end, so there is no real starting or finishing point (Figure 1-3). We can think of it as a circle with a different force dominant at five different points on it; some of these forces are more yang or downward moving, and others are more yin or upward moving. Let's intercept it near the bottom of the circle, at the point of changeover between these two types of energy—from the predominantly yang or downward-moving arc of the circle, to the more yin or upward-moving side—so we can examine each element or stage of the cycle in detail. These stages will be our first clues to our own personality traits, because each of us is influenced predominantly by one of these elements. At the same time, they're also clues to phases we all go through over time in whatever we do.

The point of transition we're looking at is known as the *water element stage*. It's a kind of floating between states—yang energy has diminished almost to nothing, and yin energy has yet to make itself felt. In terms of the Earth's seasons, this phase has the quality of midwinter: snow lies deep on the ground, but the potential for spring growth is already developing below ground, out of sight, where the dormant roots hold life force, and soon there will be steady movement toward melting of the snows.

Time passes, and we come to the stage known as *wood*. This stage is typified by the irrepressible yin energy of seedlings germinating, bulbs pushing up green spikes, sap rising in the branches, and buds bursting forth in a frenzy of sudden and rapid growth.

But this too is a passing phase, and as summer approaches, spring's persistent energy wanes. Now we enter the stage called *fire,* when the sun is hotter and the plant world blossoms into flower. The upward and outward yin energies are peaking yet even as they reach their peak, they begin to diminish. So now the energy of growth comes in more short-lived bursts that suddenly dissipate, just like the individual flames of a fire that shoot up and are gone. And so, after a short show of splendor, the petals fall.

We now pass into the second half of the overall cycle; yin is giving way to yang, and the energies of the natural world begin to settle earthward. It's late summer, the time of fruit setting in the plant realm. This is known as the *earth stage* of the transformation sequence—when the energy flows back into the soil in which plants grow.

As autumn comes, there is an ever stronger gathering of energy inward. It's the time for the plants to set seed, die back, and then gather their energies into their roots with the approach of winter. There is a pervasive sense of contraction and compaction of energies in this stage, called *metal*—an ever-increasing process of freezing and hardening—before we move into the water phase again, with its quality of floating and incipient melting.

And so the repeating cycle goes on: wood, fire, earth, metal, water, again and again, in life's complex and subtle flow of transition. No two moments are exactly alike, and yet it has always happened before.

The Nine Astrological Numbers

We've gone from identifying just two kinds of cosmic energy to distinguishing five universal types; now we are ready to go one step further, to the nine phases of influence that are at the core of sudoku astrology. We grasp these nine influences through deeper examination of the Five Elements in their cycle, and we associate their archetypal qualities with the numbers 1 to 9.

Number 9 represents the highest and most active level of energies, signified by the fire element stage. At the other extreme, the water stage is the least active and is symbolized by the number 1.

Between these two extremes, the number 5 represents the point of balance, the central point in the earth stage. But the earth element has two other substages. These are represented by the number 2, signifying earth energy that still contains a component of rising yin—more akin to fire—and number 8, which is earth energy with a more yang, inward-gathering quality, somewhat akin to metal.

The remaining two stages, wood and metal, also contain two substages each.

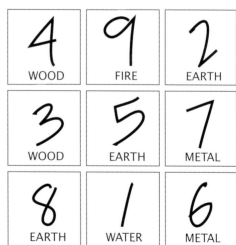

1-4. The nine numbers and their elements, arranged in a magic square.

Number 3 describes wood energies like those of early spring's most burgeoning phase, while number 4 is assigned to the slightly mellower nature of later spring.

Likewise, number 7 represents the more dramatic early autumn phase of metal energy, and number 6 has the qualities of the later phase, when energies are most gathered inward.

These characteristics will be the basis for our understanding of the personalities influenced by each number; we'll look more closely at the distinctions between them, and what these mean, in the following chapter. They also give us tools for examining the different phases of experience we all pass through over time; we'll examine these in Chapter 5.

Finally, Chinese tradition depicts these numbers arranged in a diagrammatic format that expresses the archetypal qualities assigned to each in traditional numerology, and how they relate to one another, thus producing the magic square—the foundation of sudoku astrological analysis (Figure 1-4).

In the next chapter you will discover how to read the magic square, and thus you will find out which of these influences apply to you.

Your Personality and Potential

In Chapter 1, we saw how the influences that inform sudoku astrology have been understood and used from time immemorial. We've also learned the basic nature of the nine major influences. Now it's time to discover which of these influences apply to you and to interpret what they mean.

In zodiac astrology, you can get more insights from understanding the different signs and influences and from doing your own in-depth astrological reading than from consulting a daily horoscope snippet in your local newspaper—right? It's just the same with sudoku astrology, except that I think you'll find sudoku astrology a lot easier to understand and master. With the understanding of the energy patterns that you have gained, you will be able to interpret what follows as it applies to you as a unique individual.

In zodiac astrology, each individual belongs to an overall category called a birth house, such as Libra or Pisces; he or she is then distinguished from others in the same house by more specific information, such as a rising sign. Sudoku astrology uses an analogous system of distinction—a broad grouping into nine overall personality categories or houses and then a more detailed subdivision into two further categories or aspects. All three levels of classification are expressed as numbers between 1 and 9.

THE THREE ASPECTS OF PERSONALITY

Your set of three birth numbers broadly sums up the totality of your personality, representing the astrological influences operating at your time of birth and making their imprint on you. So your astrological makeup is a subtle interplay of three influences at once, expressed as a set of three numbers—for instance, 8:4:9 or 4:3:6. The three numbers of your birth chart are termed the *year number,* the *month number,* and the *outer number.*

Let's look at the three fundamental aspects of your nature that these describe; then you'll find out how to work out your set of three numbers from your birth date; and after that you'll discover how to interpret the influences in these three different departments of your character.

The Year Number

The first influence in your makeup, your *year number,* describes the dominant energy in the year you were born. Sometimes called your *primary number,* your year number expresses the qualities you're born with, your essential makeup, your deeper nature. The qualities of this number reflect the most fundamental influences on the personal characteristics you display in important areas of life: your predominant patterns of personality, your personal values, your inclinations toward activities and pursuits, the type of career that suits you, your potential for developing over your lifetime, and so on. The year number is all about the major influences upon the way you live life in the world. It's also the single most powerful factor in how you're likely to relate to other people, and it reveals useful information about your health tendencies. As the year number has the broadest effect, it can be an important indicator for long-term aspects of relationship, which we will look at in more detail in Chapter 4.

The Month Number

The second component of your astrological makeup is your *month number,* based on the influence at work in the month you were born. The month number is sometimes known as the *character number.* This represents the qualities in you that are somewhat closer to the surface than your year-number qualities: your mental and emotional patterns and your style of communication. Although its influence is not quite as profound as the year number's influence, this second aspect is also vital in understanding your total astrological makeup. The month number is often the key element in how you respond to others in love and sexual relationships and in families, as communication and feelings are so influential in these realms.

The Outer Number

The third key element, your *outer number,* sometimes termed the *energetic number,* is a derivative of the other two and is arrived at a bit differently; you'll see how in a minute. Your outer number characterizes the aspects of your nature that are most visible or on the surface—the way you express yourself in the moment, and your minute-to-minute behavior, quirks, and habits. It's most related to how people go about their day-to-day activities. These aspects are your short-term tendencies and your patterns of reaction to immediate stimuli—the way you may appear to people who have only just met you, for instance. So your outer number represents how you can be when you're not necessarily coming from your most profound being. In other words, it's a more superficial mode. Nonetheless, it's a necessary part of your individual persona, essential to take into account in order to understand yourself and to understand others. Your outer number, too, will have a significant effect on your own experiences of life and on your relationships with others.

Generally speaking, people who meet you will tend to see the qualities belonging to your outer number first and then will come to see your month number characteristics when they know you a little better. The year number characteristics are the deepest and generally the last for newcomers to discover. Have you ever noticed how often it happens that when you've known someone for a long time, you begin to realize that he or she is quite different from the way the person first seemed? The same can even happen with self-knowledge; people may conceal certain aspects of their deeper nature from themselves until later in life, or they may not discover those aspects at all. This may stem from an unconscious need to conform to certain ideals and beliefs or it may result from pressure on the part of family, partners, peers, or friends, for instance. If you're prone to this sort of suppression, your hidden characteristics and the potential they contain may not become known to you until you've done some reflection or self-development work—or perhaps sudoku astrology.

FINDING YOUR NUMBERS

It's easy to find each of these numbers with just the most basic information about your birth. Unlike a birth chart used in Western astrology, which requires you to pinpoint your birth to the minute, sudoku astrology requires only the date. There's one important point to note: the calculations are based on the Oriental system of counting time, which is different from the system used in the West. This is because the influences being measured take into account not only solar but lunar influences, as well as the interaction of the two, as expressed in the traditional Oriental calendar. This means that the beginning of every month and of every year occurs according to the phases of the moon. The start and end dates for years and months are shown in the charts that follow.

How to Find Your Year Number

Your year number is the most straightforward to work out; it is simply the number or influence that was prevailing in your year of birth. Every year is governed by one number in an ever-repeating cycle, from 9 down to 1. Figure 2-1 gives the year numbers for all the years between 1901 and 2017. Note that the nine-number year starts about a month later than our Western year, on February 4th, so read off the number

9	8	7	6	5	4	3	2	1
1901	1902	1903	1904	1905	1906	1907	1908	1909
1910	1911	1912	1913	1914	1915	1916	1917	1918
1919	1920	1921	1922	1923	1924	1925	1926	1927
1928	1929	1930	1931	1932	1933	1934	1935	1936
1937	1938	1939	1940	1941	1942	1943	1944	1945
1946	1947	1948	1949	1950	1951	1952	1953	1954
1955	1956	1957	1958	1959	1960	1961	1962	1963
1964	1965	1966	1967	1968	1969	1970	1971	1972
1973	1974	1975	1976	1977	1978	1979	1980	1981
1982	1983	1984	1985	1986	1987	1988	1989	1990
1991	1992	1993	1994	1995	1996	1997	1998	1999
2000	2001	2002	2003	2004	2005	2006	2007	2008
2009	2010	2011	2012	2013	2014	2015	2016	2017

2-1. Find your sudoku astrology year number. All sudoku years start on February 4, so if your birth date is from January 1 through February 3, use the birth year of the previous year to the Western year. For example, if your birth date is January 29, 1965, your birth year is 1964.

for your birth year accordingly. If you were born on January 29, 1965, your birth year is 1964, for example.

Find your sudoku astrology year number by finding your birth year in Figure 2-1 and looking up at the column head for the sudoku astrology year number.

There is also a very simple formula that you can use to work out your year number without consulting Figure 2-1. Just add together the four digits of your year of birth. If this new number is greater than 10, add its two digits together to get a single-digit number. Then subtract this number from 11. The result is the year number, shown in the example below:

1947 = 1 + 9 + 4 + 7 = 21
2 + 1 = 3
11 - 3 = 8

So 1947 is an 8 year, and your sudoku astrology year number is 8.

How to Find Your Month Number

Each month is governed by a number also, in a repeating nine-month cycle from 9 down to 1. Your *month number* is the number that prevailed during the month of your birth. Figure 2-2 is a simple chart of months and their corresponding sudoku month numbers. Note again that the month does not start on the first day of our Western months. If you were born in the first few days of April, for example, your month number will be that of March for sudoku astrology purposes.

To find your month number, you need to have already worked out your sudoku astrology year number from Figure 2-1. Then find your sudoku astrology year number at the top of Figure 2-2, go down that column to the row that contains your birth date, and that will pinpoint your natal month and month number.

How to Find Your Outer Number

The way you behave on a moment-to-moment basis in everyday life is strongly influenced by your patterns of communication, thought, and feeling; by your more hidden characteristics; and by the interaction of the two as well. Correspondingly, the *outer number* is derived from the interrelationship of your first two numbers (the year number and month number). Let's look at how to determine the outer number.

In Chapter 1, you discovered the diagram known as the magic square. In point of fact, what we looked at then was only the standard form of the square, showing the arrangement of the nine numbers when they are in their home positions, which express their essence. This situation happens at the middle point of every nine-year cycle. But the arrangement changes over time. There are actually eight other magic square variations, each with a different arrangement of the numbers, which describe the arrangement of the elemental influences in each of the other years in the repeating cycle before and after the middle point. In other words, each number has its

	YEAR NUMBER		
BIRTH DATE	1 4 7	2 5 8	3 6 9
FEB 4 - MAR 5	8	2	5
MAR 6 - APR 4	7	1	4
APR 5 - MAY 5	6	9	3
MAY 6 - JUN 5	5	8	2
JUN 6 - JUL 7	4	7	1
JUL 8 - AUG 7	3	6	9
AUG 8 - SEP 7	2	5	8
SEP 8 - OCT 8	1	4	7
OCT 9 - NOV 7	9	3	6
NOV 8 - DEC 7	8	2	5
DEC 8 - JAN 5	7	1	4
JAN 6 - FEB 3	6	9	3

2-2. Use this chart to find your month number, starting with your sudoku astrology year number and reading down the top right columns to pinpoint your natal month and sudoku month number.

The nine squares in the cycle of changing influences. Refer to these squares
to find your outer number. See text for details.

own version of the magic square. Figure 2-3 shows the nine different squares that express all the years in the cycle of changing influences. We will use these nine squares again in Chapter 5 when we look at the effects of elemental energies at different points in time.

Arriving at the the outer number takes a little thinking. Your outer number is determined by the position that your year number occupies in the particular square that prevailed in your month of birth—in other words, the square that has your month number at the center. To discover the outer number, just follow these steps:

1. Find the square that has your month number in the center. (You can find your month number in Figure 2-2, as discussed above.)
2. Look for the position in the square with your month number in the center that is occupied by your year number, such as top left corner or middle of the bottom row.
3. Now look at the central magic square in Figure 2-3, the standard square, the one with 5 in the center. Find the number that occupies the position you identified in Step 2. This will be your outer number.

Here's an example of how to find your outer number. Let's say you've already discovered that your year number is 8 and your month number is 4. As shown in Figure 2-4 (left side), you first select the square that has 4 in the middle, also called the square of 4. You'll see that in this square, 8 is located in the middle of the top row. Now, looking at the 5 square, or *standard square* (shown on the right in Figure 2-4), you see that the position in the middle of the top row is occupied by number 9. So 9 is your outer number. Put together, your sudoku astrology numbers are 8:4:9 as 8 = year number, 4 = month number, and 9 = outer number.

A large number of people in the world will share exactly the same three-figure

NUMBER 8 OCCUPIES
THIS POSITION . . .

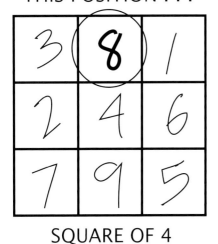

SQUARE OF 4

. . . WHICH IS KNOWN
AS 9 POSITION

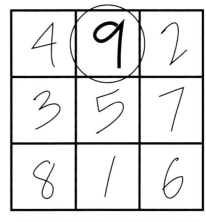

STANDARD SQUARE

2-4. An example of finding the outer number. For this person, the year number is 8 and
the month number is 4. The outer number is 9.

chart, yet each person is a unique individual, shaped by a number of other factors, which might include the effect of life experiences, parental influence and example, the environment in which the person has grown up, and so on. Perhaps the best way to look at this is to think of these other factors as a personalized filter through which the broad astrological factors work to produce your individuality. You can gain general information from the astrological analysis and then interpret it in the light of your particular circumstances and understanding of yourself. This discrimination will enable you to be empowered by astrology, rather than being limited by it or dependent on it. We'll talk more about this in the last chapter.

THE NINE TYPES OF PERSONALITY

Now let's look at what these numbers indicate about you. The information that follows describes the nine personality types. You'll see that these traits all correspond to the nine subdivisions of the Five Elements that we laid out in the previous chapter.

Each of these types has historically been represented by a classical Chinese image drawn from traditional rural or imperial life, and each has an *I Ching* trigram expressing it, showing the interaction of yin and yang for each type of energy. Each trigram is a combination of three lines, broken or unbroken. A broken line represents yin energy, and an unbroken line represents yang. You'll see the trigram and the name of the classical image at the top of each personality description.

Characteristics given here are interpretations of the nine broad types of energetic influence. From them you can gain information for the year number, or primary number, aspect of your chart. But you can use this information to understand characteristics that come from your month number (or character number) and outer number (or energetic number) as well. So if your month number is 2, then 2-type qualities will be seen in your emotional and thought patterns, and so on. Since no individual on the planet is quite the same as any other, the influences are described in broad metaphorical terms. It's up to you to work out the precise interpretation of the general traits that is appropriate for you. And by the way, always remember—no number is better than any other!

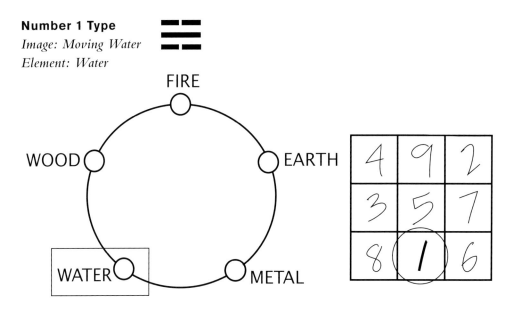

Number 1 Type
Image: Moving Water
Element: Water

2-5. Number 1 position in the cycle of Five Elements and in the magic square.

The influence that shapes the number 1 personality is the stage of the Five-Element cycle that marks the end of the descending yang movement and the beginning of the rising yin flow in the nine-year cycle, so there is a quality of floating between states (Figure 2-5). Yet the number 1 personality also reflects other, more definite attributes that are related to the distinctive qualities of moving water.

The poetic image associated with number 1 in the Oriental tradition is that of water that falls as drops on the mountaintops and then forms streams that flow rapidly downhill, merging with others to create a great river, eventually flowing into the mighty ocean. Along the way, the element of water displays many powerful attributes, such as its constant readiness for motion; its ability to sustain long and difficult journeys, always eventually reaching its ultimate destination; its ability to flow round all obstacles; its hidden depths; and its adaptability to the shape of any container.

People under the influence of this sign will possess corresponding characteristics. Within the overall category there is variation. For instance, some water people display more of the element's adventurous and youthful "mountain stream" qualities, while others reflect the idea that "still waters run deep." The number 1 type is also associated with that time of winter when the snow lies on the ground, yet preparation for spring is going on unseen among the plant bulbs and tree roots. This image implies the potential for inner or spiritual strength that may go unnoticed until the right time comes in the order of things.

We begin to get a picture of the type's broad characteristics, even though their precise form varies from person to person. Water people are usually sociable and outgoing, with many acquaintances. They tend to be easygoing or even serene, adaptable and eager to please rather than to cause any trouble. If an individual hasn't developed these qualities in a positive way, they may appear instead as indecisiveness, lack of direction, or a tendency to be easily swayed. There are hidden emotional depths to water, a certain mystery, and it's often difficult for others to tell what's going on in water people's minds. Though generally sociable, they can also enjoy solitude, and are often familiar with the world of spirituality and the invisible. They are usually patient, but can worry unnecessarily.

Love can present challenges. Water people have strong sexual desires and enjoy intimacy, but they're sometimes scared about getting hurt, and they may become insecure if this has happened to them already. In other areas, such as career or personal development, their own success can be enhanced by the friendship, partnership, mentoring, or the beneficial influence of another person.

Examples of people with year number 1:

- Eric Clapton
- Nelson Mandela
- Andy Warhol
- Charles Darwin
- Van Morrison
- Clark Gable
- Queen Victoria

Number 2 Type

Image: Mother Earth
Element: Earth

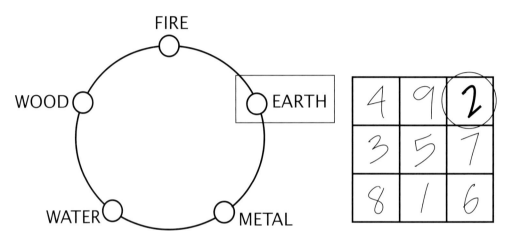

2-6. Number 2 position in the cycle of Five Elements and in the magic square.

The natural image associated with this influence is that of Mother Earth, traditionally seen as accepting energies given from the universe, nourishing and embracing life on the planet, along with providing all the sustained input of time and hard work that this implies (Figure 2-6).

People born with number 2 as their year influence inherit broadly corresponding qualities. They are usually patient and diligent, often thoughtful and reserved, but persistent in the face of difficulty. They enjoy helping and nourishing others, even when they themselves are in a leadership capacity. Number 2 people of either gender have a strong feminine aspect, although it is not necessarily revealed in public. These people are perceptive of other people's characters and sensitive to their problems, and they can make others feel at ease.

In relationships, number 2 people can be devoted and attentive to their partners' needs, but may tend to be reticent or overly conciliatory. They like to have another person there to receive all that nourishing from them. Some may need to watch out for a tendency to self-sacrifice. Though meticulous, they are stronger on ideals and aspirations than on the practical application of their ideas. They are more inclined to be conservative than unconventional.

Examples of people with year number 2:

- Tony Blair
- Allen Ginsberg
- Marilyn Monroe
- The Dalai Lama
- David Lean
- Alfred Hitchcock
- Indira Gandhi
- George Lucas

Number 3 Type
Image: Thunder
Element: Wood

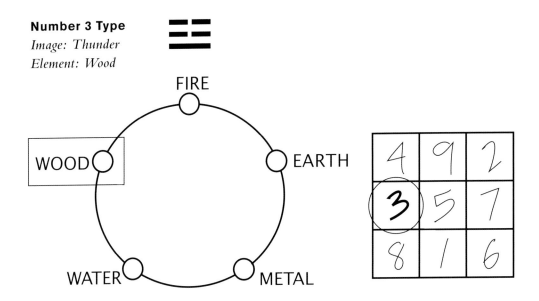

2-7. Number 3 position in the cycle of Five Elements and in the magic square.

The number 3 type embodies the first energies of early spring: the unstoppability of new growth, the sense of rebirth and renewal, the quality of a young tree whose branches reach up enthusiastically but whose roots are not yet deep (Figure 2-7). The *I Ching* trigram describing this type evokes thunder's sudden, explosive energy and the bursts of lightning that accompany it, illuminating the whole sky. Corresponding personal qualities include acute sensitivity, vibrancy, and an urgent sense of quest for life's new experiences.

Indeed, the 3 type person is spontaneously interested in all kinds of different activities and experiences, in living for pleasure, and in enjoying movement and action. Possessing the spirit of youth, this person tends to be ambitious, humorous, independent, sociable, and idealistic. At the same time, those influences, if not channeled positively, may make him or her hasty or rash, unpredictable, quick to change, not terribly practical, and a rather superficial thinker. Determination is definitely there, but it may not be accompanied by the patience to follow projects through to the end. This person may be tempted to move on instead to the "next big thing."

The sexual drive of number 3 is usually strong and impulsive, like nature's need to release the pent-up energies of spring, although if this seems just too strong for the individual, it may be suppressed.

In relationships, 3 is usually positive, open, and honest, but sensitive enough to be easily hurt; communicative, but sometimes brutally frank. His or her bursts of passionate energy can be a great asset in relationships with some partners, but to others these outbursts may seem a bit too much. The 3 person would therefore be well advised to cultivate the ability to pay attention and listen to other people.

Examples of people with year number 3:

- Jimmy Connors
- Mick Jagger
- Robin Williams
- Adolf Hitler
- Robert de Niro
- Kate Hudson
- Meg Ryan

Number 4 Type

Image: The Wind

Element: Wood

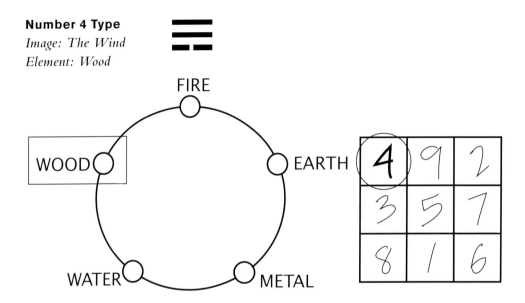

2-8. Number 4 position in the cycle of Five Elements and in the magic square.

This second type within the element of wood corresponds to the energies of later spring, when the drive of growth and expansion is more dispersed (Figure 2-8). This sign is also associated with the wind; many personal qualities derive from this. From person to person and moment to moment, this wind can vary from the gentlest of breezes—indicating qualities of tenderness and affection—to the powerful emotions symbolized by a raging gale. And along the way there may be wind-like changes in direction, turbulence of feelings, and lack of clarity or singleness of purpose.

The compassionate and loving aspects of the number 4 type manifest particularly in relationships and social settings, where there is an innate desire to take care of others.

Number 4 people have a strong desire for things to be harmonious, romantic, or even sentimental, which can sometimes border on naiveté. With very high ideals in these matters, number 4 people may sometimes feel let down or hurt by others who don't seem to meet their standards.

Communication and intuition are usually strong points. Number 4 is also easygoing and often charismatic. But if these qualities are not cultivated in a positive way, they may develop into tendencies to indecision, acting on impulse or whim, changes of mind, and lack of consistent willpower. Number 4 people can also be taken in by others and may give their trust inappropriately or be overly influenced by those around them. They should take care to develop the capacity for self-assertiveness and self-reliance. But if they don't, never mind—when things go wrong, these people can always bounce back and succeed next time!

Examples of people with year number 4:

- Kenneth Branagh
- Martin Scorsese
- Joan Collins
- Rudolf Steiner
- Jimi Hendrix
- Orson Welles

Number 5 Type

Image: Central Power
Element: Earth

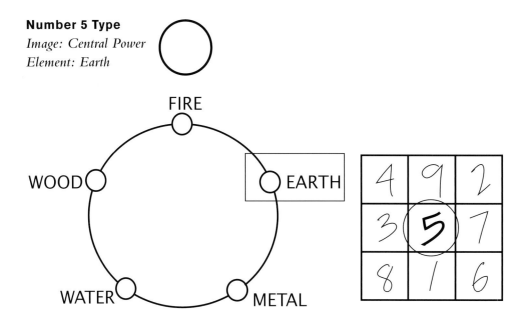

2-9. Number 5 position in the cycle of Five Elements and in the magic square.

The number 5 sign is traditionally associated with the centralized power of the king or emperor, the holder of primal power in the land, who balances opposites and extremes—the great controller who possesses both highly creative and highly destructive potential. More than all the other numbers, number 5 people have great scope for how they develop their potential and what effect they will have on those around them.

As we have seen from the magic square (Figure 2-9), the 5 character stands alone, distinctly central, while all the other numbers connect together and support one another in a circular pattern around it. This is the clue to all of number 5's distinctive characteristics. This person is perfectly capable of influencing and organizing all the other personalities and is very much used to being at the center of things. Often acting with strength and boldness, he or she can be enormously helpful and supportive, a positive influence on others, but can also be egotistical, manipulative, or inconsiderate. Likewise, this person is likely to undergo extreme and often unexpected experiences in life—big highs, big lows, and big turnarounds. Luckily, he or she is very well equipped to deal with all this and more, enduring failures, hardships, or crises that might destroy other mortals.

In relationships, the need to maintain a kingly show of strength and emotional self-sufficiency can get in the way of ordinary needs such as affection, and so 5s tend to have fewer really close, intimate friends, but many of them are perfectly happy this way. Either way, the 5 will enjoy being a center of attention. His or her very direct expression of opinions can be tactless and may hurt a partner who is less robust. The extremes to which 5s gravitate—moral or immoral, ambitious or lazy, creative or destructive, with no middle way—can also be difficult for partners to deal with. People in relationships with 5s may therefore find themselves subject to some of the same extreme ups and downs.

Examples of people with year number 5:

- Ludwig van Beethoven
- Celine Dion
- Liv Tyler
- Orlando Bloom
- Mahatma Gandhi
- Simon Cowell
- Guy Ritchie

Number 6 Type

Image: Heaven

Element: Metal

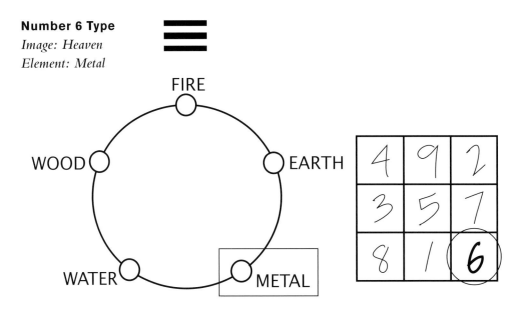

2-10. Number 6 position in the cycle of Five Elements and in the magic square.

The qualities of number 6 type are represented by the time of harvest, with its strong sense of energies gathering inwards. The trigram summarizing this character symbolizes heaven, in the Oriental sense—as the active creative principle of the universe—evoking personal qualities of order, constancy, perfection, organization, discipline, and completeness. On the other side of this coin is the potential for rigidity, pride, or inflexible will. It's all very *yang*. The number 6 person is inclined to noble attitudes and high ideals, with plenty of inner strength and courage, and is prepared to take risks on matters of principle. The number 6's position in the cycle of the Five Elements and his or her magic square are shown in Figure 2-10.

The 6 mind is efficient and calculating, persistent and strong-willed, ready to con-quer any obstacle. Number 6s are also idealistic and have a strong moral stance. They aren't so good at being spontaneous and in the moment.

The number 6 person is also strong on family values and usually is loyal, but often is able to dominate a partner. He or she does not like to be the loser (or even the sub-ordinate), has difficulty with criticism, and can seem emotionally reserved or even somewhat cold. Partners of 6s usually do well to let them take the lead (or let them think so, anyway!).

He or she can be guilty of using other people to his or her own ends and may have difficulty focusing attention outward, away from the self and toward others. The tendency to stubbornness and lack of adaptability can also be a factor in relationship situations. The 6 person is therefore advised to allow a little *yin* energy into his or her life: to cultivate a modicum of selflessness, warmth, and consideration for others; to practice listening; and to let other people have what they want even when the 6 *knows* what would really be better for them! When this aspect is taken care of, the influence of 6 can be a strong and positive influence in any situation.

Examples of people with year number 6:

- Kurt Cobain
- John Lennon
- Sharon Stone
- Mikhail Gorbachev
- Madonna
- Reese Witherspoon
- Nicole Kidman
- Richard Nixon

Number 7 Type

Image: Harvest

Element: Metal

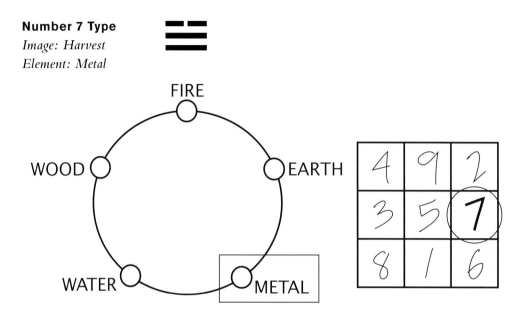

2-11. Number 7 position in the cycle of Five Elements and in the magic square.

The image from the natural world that represents this sign is the celebration of harvest time, the fruitfulness of autumn, and material plenty. This implies human qualities of joyfulness, pleasure, entertainment, celebration, and material gain, with a penchant for fashion, dining out, entertaining friends, holding dinner parties—all key concepts in the number 7 person's worldview.

The symbolism of the harvest, a time when people could pause from their labors and take time to think, leads us to the reflective inner aspect and mental sharpness that are key attributes of the 7 metal type, coupled—and contrasted—with a potentially hedonistic exterior. Chinese tradition considers this sign to be the most fortunate of all signs; but we must remember that Chinese astrology has long placed special emphasis on purely material prosperity. The position in the cycle of Five Elements and in the magic square for number 7 people are shown in Figure 2-11.

Number 7 people, then, are competent at managing their business and personal affairs—and those of others. They work hard and then enjoy the fruits of their labor with equal dedication—like spending money, for instance! They diligently pursue happiness and enjoyment.

They are generally optimistic, but can sometimes be moody, perhaps oscillating between joyfulness and introspection. In relationships, they are intuitive and sensitive to the moods of others—which is very valuable—but sometimes prone to using this ability in a calculating or self-interested way. Number 7s can be very sincere, charming, and persuasive. They want to be loved, and they may be overly interested in self-validation. All too often, though, they are resistant when change is needed to make things work—unless, of course, it's the other person who's going to do the changing! They are eager to be free and unconstrained by others and are cautious about becoming committed to long-term relationships. But they are respectful, and they make good people to confide in.

Relations with the opposite sex are of fundamental importance to 7s. They should choose lovers carefully—with the heart rather than the head—and beware of their potential arrogance, cultivating sensitivity and emotional generosity instead, in order to make the best of relationships.

Examples of people with year number 7:

- Prince Charles
- Mike Tyson
- Francis Ford Coppola
- Andrew Lloyd Webber
- Michelle Pfeiffer

Number 8 Type

Image: The Mountain
Element: Earth

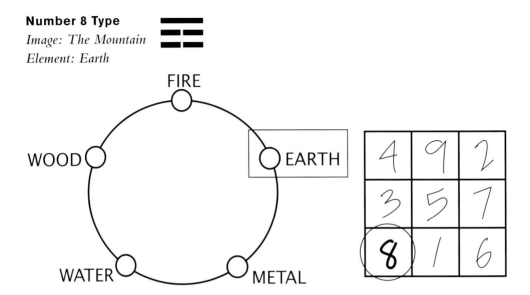

2-12. Number 8 position in the cycle of Five Elements and in the magic square.

Of the three earth signs, this is the most *yang,* the most inwardly directed. The essence of 8 is found in the mountain that rises above everything else, unmoving and immovable, offering far-reaching views from its peak. In human terms this translates into qualities such as firmness, stability, tenacity, and a far-reaching perspective on life, along with corresponding potential weaknesses: stubbornness, pride, haughtiness, and the risk of loneliness or isolation.

Number 8s have strong powers of concentration and think deeply about things—indeed, they sometimes think too much—and they hold carefully reasoned points of view, which they may be slow to let go of. They gradually learn life skills over time, steadily accumulating learning and lessons from their experiences, rather than developing in an impulsive way. These people can be resistant to change.

Number 8's relationships can benefit from the virtues of determination, endurance, and strength of mind and will, but this same will can often be imposed on others—to their detriment. Ego and high self-esteem can often lead the 8 to think of self first. Number 8s have strong emotions and desires, but don't always express or show them, so they often resist advances and can be hard to get to know.

Although obstinate on the outside, however, they are usually more soft, gentle, and yielding underneath. They are generally steady, reliable, trustworthy, and honest in relationships and are able to be faithful and constant in partnerships, in which their inner strength is a considerable asset. The potential habit of thinking about things excessively may also lead to less desirable emotional responses, such as jealousy of others.

Number 8s can be very private, particularly with their sexual identity and its outward expression, which can sometimes lead to repression. When things do work out right, though, they are capable of finding deep fulfillment. The position in the cycle of Five Elements and in the magic square for number 8s are shown in Figure 2-12.

Examples of people with year number 8:

- Yasser Arafat
- Ronald Reagan
- Steven Spielberg
- Queen Elizabeth
- Marquis de Sade
- Martin Luther King, Jr.
- O. J. Simpson

Number 9 Type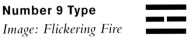
Image: Flickering Fire
Element: Fire

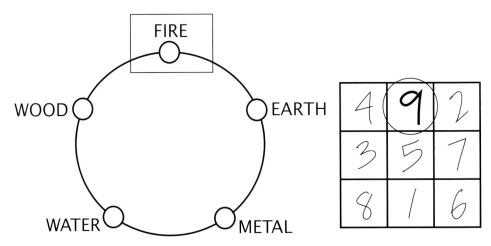

2-13. Number 9 position in the cycle of Five Elements and in the magic square.

This sign is represented by the archetypal image of the summer sun and the nature of fire itself—its brightness and clarity, its attractive and hypnotic flame, its burning frenzy and the heat that it radiates, its flickering and ultimate return to quietness as each individual flame exhausts itself and dies down.

Number 9 people generally display qualities of brilliance and love to be the star. They are attracted to fame and success and have a strong interest in matters of beauty and taste. External appearances are important to them. As they follow their path in life, they shine a light for both themselves and others. At the same time, they can be fickle and vain, impatient and inconstant. Underneath their hot, passionate surface there can be a cooler core.

Number 9 people are active, with intense but short-lived bursts of energy. They make contact with a great number of people, though most of these friendships and relationships are not profound. They like to do many different things, but can lack singleness of purpose or perseverance in following through to completion.

In matters of relationship, 9 people are lively, outgoing and sociable, naturally attractive to others, and good at attracting attention to themselves. They are passionate, emotionally expressive, excitable and affectionate—quick to anger, but also quick to calm down again. They are generally good communicators. However, they often proceed impulsively, sometimes without regard for others.

Number 9s seem to be able to attract people without even trying. They are very romantic; love is extremely important to them. However, because they can easily feel trapped, they may have difficulty with commitment. For the best relationships, 9 types would do well to develop self-control and persistence and avoid undue influence from stronger individuals. The number 9's position in the cycle of Five Elements and in the magic square are shown in Figure 2-13.

Examples of people with year number 9:

- Cher
- Victor Hugo
- Robert Redford
- Walt Disney
- Saddam Hussein
- Mother Teresa
- Bill Gates
- Liza Minnelli

WHAT THE NINE TYPES MEAN FOR YOU

Now that you know the characteristics of the nine types, you can use them to interpret the three categories of your chart representing your *year number,* your *month number,* and your *outer number.*

A Sample Chart

Let's look again at the example from the beginning of this chapter where we worked out a person's three numbers. The numbers were:

Year number: 8
Month number: 4
Outer number: 9

We summarized this as 8:4:9.

This person—let's say it's a man—has a dominant energy of the 8 "mountain" type, interwoven with the influences of 4 and 9. He will, for sure, have 8's qualities of farsight-edness, stability, and tenaciousness in major departments of his life. If he's not careful, he may see the other side of that coin as well—the tendency to stubbornness, the pride and desire for status, the sense of superiority that can lead to isolation. He will be able to think deeply and concentrate strongly—sometimes too strongly and too deeply.

He will put great energy into building up his life determinedly over time, methodi-cally putting elaborate plans into practice. He may well be one of those late starters who gets the hang of things later in life by trial and error, but who doesn't forget any of the lessons he's learned and by midlife knows how to be happy. His sexuality will pri-marily stem from this part of his character, which may not make for the most dynamic sexual expressiveness.

Yet at the same time the far more ephemeral energy of 9 in his surface nature strongly tinges this underlying pattern. For example, it may produce a habit of sorting things out on a moment-to-moment basis, which may compromise his number 8 qualities of wisdom and capacity for foresight. So the calm steadiness may give way to spontaneity, quick decisions, or mercurial changes of mind until he returns to his deeper and better judgment.

Under the influence of his month number, there will be an irrepressible and optimistic quality in this person's thinking and his emotional response to life, stemming from the spring-like energies of 4. This influence could also manifest in his approach to spiritual matters and "the meaning of life." It may not be noticeable to casual acquaintances, but those who are closest to him will become aware of it from subtle signs, and they may well be inspired and uplifted by that positive influence. The 4 energy operating at an inner level may also make this person's intuition extremely strong—something of great value if it is trusted, cultivated, and brought to bear on ordinary life. The wood element energies of 4, combined with the nourishing potential of the 8 earth, indicate motivation toward compassion and interest in taking care of others—but only when the mountain is inclined, and not so much when he is in aloof or detached mode!

In relationships, this person would do well to draw on his deeper resources of judgment (the 8 and 4 rather than 9 reserves) when making major decisions or taking important actions. Acting from the more spontaneous 9 nature—for instance, falling in love and wanting to marry someone on the spur of the moment—would not be a good idea.

In communication, he needs to be aware that the merits of his well-thought-out plans and visions will not always be so self-evident to those around him who possess less insight or less sense of perspective. So he should take care to spell things out to others—without arrogance, if possible. Communication about his wants, needs, and feelings will also require special effort in any intimate relationship. But this person's capacity for commitment, focus, and persistence can help make the right relationship something really special.

Health and Physical Constitution

Every element has a range of "correspondences," or aspects of the physical world it relates to and resonates with, shown in Figure 2-14. So your year number and the element that belongs to it can also be useful pointers to certain aspects of your constitutional health—the health orientation that you were born with. This does *not* mean being born with good health or bad health; it means that since one particular element is your "native" or strongest element, a certain organ system in your body corresponding to that element will be inherently strongest at birth. There is also a corresponding season and time of day when this organ is at its most important or when problems may manifest, as well as particular foods and particular tastes that are helpful in supporting its health.

There's one possible downside to having one organ system constitutionally stronger than the others: you may unconsciously exploit that strength by overdoing things that will harm it. This can happen because the strongest system will tolerate more abuse than the others before you notice things starting to go wrong.

For instance, a wood element person will have a strong liver and gallbladder system, and so will be better able to tolerate stress to that system for a long time, such as eating too much fatty food or drinking excessive alcohol, apparently without too much effect. But once this damage is done and signs are starting to appear, it will take longer to recover because it has gone on longer and worked deeper. Other systems, inherently not quite so robust in that person, will draw attention by giving signs when they're being harmed. The stomach system, for instance, might protest quickly if a wood person puts pressure

ELEMENT	SEASON	TIME OF DAY	ORGAN SYSTEM	FOOD TASTE
WATER 1	WINTER	NIGHT	KIDNEY/BLADDER	SALT
WOOD 3, 4	SPRING	MORNING	LIVER/GALLBLADDER	SOUR
FIRE 9	HIGH SUMMER	NOON	HEART/CIRCULATION AND METABOLISM/SMALL INTESTINE	BITTER
EARTH 2, 5, 8	LATE SUMMER	AFTERNOON	STOMACH/SPLEEN PANCREAS	SWEET
METAL 6, 7	FALL	EVENING	LUNG/LARGE INTESTINE	SPICY

2-14. The elements and their correspondences.

on it by eating too much, too late in the evening, or eating foods that are too rich—something an earth element person might seem to be getting away with for years.

You can also use the information in Figure 2-14 as a starting point for strategies to deal with different health systems in the body, not just those belonging to your home element. For instance, for people of all elements, liver problems tend to be more evident in the spring, when the liver is discharging toxins accumulated in the winter. And many of the foods that are helpful to the liver have a sour taste, like sauerkraut, or are associated with spring, like spring greens and spring onions. Likewise, the kidneys can suffer in winter and are much affected by the salt balance of the blood.

USING THIS INFORMATION WISELY

Please interpret all the information in this chapter with wisdom and common sense. Remember that there is always a degree of generalization in astrological analysis, and each individual on the planet has a degree of uniqueness. Many people will share your three-number sudoku astrology configuration, yet each is a distinct individual, subject to a whole range of other factors that shape his or her character. You'll need to interpret your chart in the light of what you know about yourself.

Going through life, it's also important to develop a wide range of qualities and strengths, not just those of your type. The astrological information here can point out which of these areas are likely to be more challenging for you, but no less worthwhile, and help you work with them more effectively.

Rather than just finding out about your own type, try to understand all the types and learn how the Five-Element system works; this will help you get the most from the system, especially when you look at how things change over time.

Above all, be yourself, and be true to yourself. We'll consider this further in Chapter 6. But in the meantime, let's consider the characteristics of the people around you and learn a few shortcuts to figuring out what makes them tick.

CHAPTER

3

The People around You

In Chapter 2, you discovered how to work out your own sudoku astrology chart, summarized in the three key numbers that symbolize the influences operating at the time of your birth. In this chapter, you will see how to apply the same principles to another person.

You may wish to use this information in a number of different ways. For instance, you might want to gain a better insight into the astrological makeup of someone that you're already in relationship with. This doesn't apply just to love or romance, but to relationships of all kinds, with family members, friends, work colleagues, and anyone else whom you see often or who is important in your life. In this case, the information here may help you understand seeming contradictions within the other person's behavior and get a perspective on his or her personality—such as which elements of his or her makeup are fundamental and which are more superficial. Then it will be easier to make the most of your relationship's potential for both of you.

Alternatively, you may want to evaluate *potential* relationship partners—for instance, romantic prospects. If you can quickly assess the temperament of someone you've just met, maybe you can get to know that person a bit more quickly, profoundly, and painlessly. For example, you may wish to know in advance how romantic the person is likely to be, and how he or she is likely to express it. Will intimacy be daunting for him or her? Is this person likely to be strong on commitment? Or might he or she want to have half a dozen other lovers in tow, as well as yourself? And will the person turn out to be the sort who can keep deep, dark secrets from you for years and years? Examining the prospect's magic square chart can point to such answers.

Maybe you don't have anyone in mind at the moment, but just want to have some indications in order to narrow down the field a bit! This may not sound like the most effective way to approach the search for a deep and meaningful soul-mate relationship, but I do recommend it as a good way for you to practice using this astrological method—tuning in to the influences that are affecting people, learning to distinguish the different types. This will not only help you develop your intuitive ability in the interest of better relationships, but also will sensitize you to the energies at work in your own life.

HOW TO WORK OUT ANOTHER PERSON'S CHART

1. Start with the Person's Birth Date

If you can obtain the person's date of birth—by fair means or foul—then you can work out his or her sudoku astrology profile just as you did your own in Chapter 2. The steps set out here will serve as a convenient refresher.

If you don't know the birth date, you can still use what you know about the nine personality types to gain valuable insight into someone else's character and behavior. We'll see how later in this chapter.

2. Work Out the Person's Year Number

To find the year number, consult Figure 3-1 or use the shortcut you learned in Chapter 2: Add together the four digits of the year of birth. If this new number is greater

9	8	7	6	5	4	3	2	1
1901	1902	1903	1904	1905	1906	1907	1908	1909
1910	1911	1912	1913	1914	1915	1916	1917	1918
1919	1920	1921	1922	1923	1924	1925	1926	1927
1928	1929	1930	1931	1932	1933	1934	1935	1936
1937	1938	1939	1940	1941	1942	1943	1944	1945
1946	1947	1948	1949	1950	1951	1952	1953	1954
1955	1956	1957	1958	1959	1960	1961	1962	1963
1964	1965	1966	1967	1968	1969	1970	1971	1972
1973	1974	1975	1976	1977	1978	1979	1980	1981
1982	1983	1984	1985	1986	1987	1988	1989	1990
1991	1992	1993	1994	1995	1996	1997	1998	1999
2000	2001	2002	2003	2004	2005	2006	2007	2008
2009	2010	2011	2012	2013	2014	2015	2016	2017

3-1. Find the year number (remember, years start on February 4).

than 10, add its two digits together to get a single-digit number. Then subtract this number from 11. The result is the year number. For example:

$$1947 = 1 + 9 + 4 + 7 = 21$$
$$2 + 1 = 3$$
$$11 - 3 = 8$$

So 1947 is an 8 year.

Remember that the sudoku year begins on February 4, not January 1, so if the birth date is between January 1 and February 3, it belongs in the previous year. For example, January 26, 1957 counts as 1956.

3. Work Out the Month Number

Once you have the year number, it's simple to find the month number, using the chart in Figure 3-2.

4. Work Out the Outer Number

Find the square that has the month number in the center and note which position in this square is occupied by the year number

YEAR NUMBER			
BIRTH DATE	1 4 7	2 5 8	3 6 9
FEB 4 - MAR 5	8	2	5
MAR 6 - APR 4	7	1	4
APR 5 - MAY 5	6	9	3
MAY 6 - JUN 5	5	8	2
JUN 6 - JUL 7	4	7	1
JUL 8 - AUG 7	3	6	9
AUG 8 - SEP 7	2	5	8
SEP 8 - OCT 8	1	4	7
OCT 9 - NOV 7	9	3	6
NOV 8 - DEC 7	8	2	5
DEC 8 - JAN 5	7	1	4
JAN 6 - FEB 3	6	9	3

3-2. Find the month number, using the birth date and year number.

(e.g., the top left corner or middle of the bottom row; Figure 3-3). Then look at the standard square, the one with 5 in the center, and find the number that occupies the same position. This is the outer number.

3	8	1
2	**4**	6
7	9	5

8	4	6
7	**9**	2
3	5	1

1	6	8
9	**2**	4
5	7	3

2	7	9
1	**3**	5
6	8	4

4	9	2
3	**5**	7
8	1	6

6	2	4
5	**7**	9
1	3	8

7	3	5
6	**8**	1
2	4	9

9	5	7
8	**1**	3
4	6	2

5	1	3
4	**6**	8
9	2	7

3-3. Refer to these squares to find the outer number.

5. Interpret the Numbers

You now have a three-number chart for the person you hope to understand, such as 8:4:9 or 2:2:5. Remember:

- The year number, or primary number, represents the way the nine types of influence appear in the person's deeper nature—the major underlying influences on how he or she lives life in the world.
- The month number, or character number, represents the qualities that are somewhat more evident in worldly life—emotional and communicative patterns.
- The outer number represents the aspects that are most visible on the surface and how one expresses oneself in spontaneous behavior and work habits.

Below, for easy reference, you'll find a summary of the characteristics associated with each type, which we explored in the last chapter.

THE NINE CHARACTER TYPES IN REVIEW

1. MOVING WATER: Water Element

POTENTIAL STRENGTHS

- Readiness for motion and ability to get around obstacles
- Independence, creating own path in life
- Hardworking, patient in difficulties, aptitude for concentration
- Intuition is important
- Emotional depths, strong sexual desires
- Sociable—but can enjoy solitude
- Usually gets there in the end

POTENTIAL CHALLENGES

- Easily swayed
- Careful, can worry unnecessarily
- Potential for obstinacy, can get in a rut
- May appear emotionally cool

2. MOTHER EARTH: Earth Element

POTENTIAL STRENGTHS

- Motherly or feminine quality
- Receptivity, tact, and diplomacy
- Nourishing, supportive, perceptive of others' needs
- Sense of service; dedicated, diligent
- Often reserved and gentle, harmonious
- Modest, takes quiet and effective action
- Strong on detail, interested in completing things

POTENTIAL CHALLENGES

- Stronger on ideals and aspirations than on practicalities
- Can be self-sacrificing
- Can be reticent or insecure
- Conservative tendency

3. THUNDER: Wood Element

POTENTIAL STRENGTHS

- Explosive energy, active vitality, brightness and vibrancy
- Outgoing, generally irrepressible and optimistic
- Curious, interested in growth; needs sense of progress

- Quick to change, restless quest for experience and experiment
- Varied talents, aesthetic values
- Sensual, romantic
- Acute sensitivity, especially to sound and music

POTENTIAL CHALLENGES
- Ambitious
- Quick to change, unpredictable, independent
- Superficial, overlooking practicalities
- Impatient, can be hasty or rash, short-tempered
- Sensitive and easily hurt, yet can be brutally frank

4. THE WIND: Wood Element
POTENTIAL STRENGTHS
- Strong sense of movement in life, many changes
- Talkative, good at communicating and disseminating information
- Quick of perception and intuition
- Adaptable, able to bounce back from any failure
- Artistically oriented
- Affectionate and romantic, often charismatic

POTENTIAL CHALLENGES
- Subject to changes of mind, scattering of energy, impulsiveness
- Impulsive, influenced by emotion, subject to influence of others, can be taken in
- Turbulent emotions or moodiness; can be confused
- Naive, can be impractical in love
- Indecision can cause confusion and shake usual confidence

5. CENTRAL POWER: Earth Element

POTENTIAL STRENGTHS

- Being at the center of things; influence and responsibility
- Bold, forceful, enjoying power
- Organizing others
- Ability to cope with extreme experiences
- Seeming emotional self-sufficiency, enduring hardships
- Inner reconciliation of opposites

POTENTIAL CHALLENGES

- Given to extremes
- Has both creative and destructive ability
- Controlling of self and others; likes to be center of attention
- Egotistical, insensitive to others' vulnerability, tactless

6. HEAVEN: Metal Element

POTENTIAL STRENGTHS

- Order, perfection, organization, clarity of purpose
- Self-esteem, discipline, inner strength, courage
- Independent, seeking completeness
- Willpower, leadership, ability to dominate
- Able to accumulate material possessions
- High ideals, constancy, dignity
- Intellect
- Exemplary behavior, reliability

POTENTIAL CHALLENGES
- Focus on self
- Rigidity; slow to take advice or criticism
- Calculating mind, can be manipulative
- Proud, not enjoying subordinate position, likes to dominate
- Emotionally cool, turned inward rather than sociable

7. HARVEST: Metal Element

POTENTIAL STRENGTHS
- Material and financial acquisitions; enjoying spending
- Hard work and then relaxation; seeking enjoyment
- Competence, resourcefulness, fluency in writing
- Values freedom
- Sharp mind, good adviser
- Respectful and loyal, easy to confide in
- Persuasive, skilled at pleasing
- Strong passions and attractions, sexual relations very important
- Most productive in later life

POTENTIAL CHALLENGES
- Outward appearances important; likes showing off, hedonistic
- Changeable temperament
- Self-interested, nervous about commitment
- Strong outside but cautious inside
- Talking rather than listening

8. MOUNTAIN: Earth Element

POTENTIAL STRENGTHS

- Far-reaching perspective
- Enjoying stability
- Self-reflective; strength of mind, powers of concentration
- Self-motivated, tenacious, and persistent
- Orderly and patient
- Faithful, steady, and trustworthy
- Able to accumulate wealth

POTENTIAL CHALLENGES

- High-minded or isolated, seeming distant
- May think too much; not verbally expressive, hard to know
- Can be stubborn, immovable, resistant to change
- Cautious in relationships, may hide emotions and desires

9. FLICKERING FIRE: Fire Element

POTENTIAL STRENGTHS

- Bright intelligence
- Versatile
- Energy in bursts
- Outgoing and sociable, enjoying involvement in things
- Drawn to fame and success
- Flamboyant, eager to communicate; wide circle of contacts

POTENTIAL CHALLENGES

- Emptiness after exhaustion
- Concerned with attractiveness, can be vain

• Quick changes of emotion; impatient
• Impulsive, dislikes constraints, lacking self-control
• Focusing on short term rather than long term

For more detailed analysis, refer back to pages 26–43 in Chapter 2. Remember that these are broad principles and influences; they will show up in somewhat different ways in different individuals.

Remember, too, the three different ways that the numbers show up in personality and behavior. If you interact with someone daily, but never talk about anything more important than the weather, for instance, what you see is probably his or her month number at work. If you're meeting someone for the first time and going purely on first impressions, it's probably his or her outer number influence that you're experiencing. And if the two of you go way back and real deep, then you're getting glimpses of his or her year number state.

RECOGNIZING THE TYPES

In the last chapter you learned how to read your own sudoku astrology chart and recognize which of the Five Elements and the nine influences are at work in your own life. Now you can experiment with interpreting the charts of people you know reasonably well. As you do, you'll start to get a real feeling for how these influences show up in people around you and how to discern their effects. Then you may be able to guess which elements and which numbers are at play in individuals around you *without* knowing their birth date. Not only is this fun—and not only might it help you meet someone you'd like to get to know a whole lot better—but it's also an excellent way of tuning into the system of energetic influences and developing your sensitivity to them.

You can find opportunities to practice this wherever you are. Spotting the five different element types is a good way to start. At work, for instance, you may come to realize that your longtime boss, who is extremely well organized but has never given much away about what's going on inside, is actually showing metal influence. At a nightclub, you might recognize that the high-energy-but-only-in-bursts DJ is a classic example of fire energy. In the coffee shop, that gentle-looking person who's been quietly giving you the eye for a while, but not doing much about it, may well be of the earth type.

If someone strikes you as a straightforward, consistent person, it's likely that his or her three numbers contain only one or two elements among them. When people's numbers contain three different elements, especially if the elements conflict, they often seem more complex and perhaps enigmatic to us, because we tend to want to see others as being of one recognizable type.

Parties are an especially good place to practice. All the clues are there—the way people sit or stand; how they interact with those around them; their vocal expression (fluid? fiery? or with a metallic edge?). Take the way people dance, for instance— one of the most revealing indicators of all. Look at the people on the dance floor. First of all, practice distinguishing the yins from the yangs; which ones are moving, literally, with more "up" energy, and which with more "down"? This is the first clue. Then break it down further and start spotting the elements. Fire style dancing tends to be the wildest, most communicative and exhibitionistic. Wood dancers also have a strong upward energy, with a more steady, irrepressible flow. Earth dancing has more of a grounded quality; metal tends to be more self-contained, the body taking more compact shapes and the arms generally kept lower. And in between, of course, is the floating, flowing water.

With further practice, you'll soon be able to go further and begin to spot the particular energy qualities of the nine numbers—the reserve or seeming aloofness of number 8, the mountain; the noisy number 4, thunder; or the restrained but distinctly sexual messages of number 7, harvest. After a while, you'll find that this whole process will become less analytical, and you'll naturally pick up on a "certain something"—that very particular energy quality—that characterizes each number.

Be careful, though, how you use this information about other people. It's one thing to understand those around you better; it's quite another to dispense unsolicited "readings" to all and sundry. Few people will appreciate you figuring out their numbers, and then marching up to them saying, "Hey, guess what! You're extremely controlling, terrified of relationships, sexually overconfident, impractical . . . " Most people don't enjoy being pigeonholed, even if you're assigning them stellar qualities. It's probably better to keep your findings to yourself for the most part—and keep an open mind.

The Magic Square and Your Relationships

You now know how to work out the set of three magic square numbers for yourself and for any other person. From these figures, you know how to interpret many indicators of your personality, potential, and general approach to life. This information can be valuable in examining any kind of relationship, whether it's in the field of friendship, family, work, or any other sphere—especially the intimate interaction of romance, which we'll focus on in this chapter.

The three-number profile in itself contains many indicators of potential compatibility and has probably already given you some clues about the dynamics of your interaction. For instance, one of you may be a wildly hedonistic party animal, while the other is a shy, retiring hermit whose main interest is spiritual withdrawal from the sensory world. This sort of comparison is simply common sense—which, of course, plays an important part in astrological investigation. However, the magic square system of sudoku astrology goes a lot further than common sense. Whether you wish to understand an existing relationship more deeply or to check out the possibilities of a new prospect, it offers some simple, powerful, and fascinating techniques for analyzing in greater depth the interacting energies of two individuals.

Compatibility has many different aspects—sexual compatibility, romantic style, communication patterns, social preferences, basic lifestyle, even broad outlook on life—that govern how one individual will function in intimacy with another. All these aspects together form a web of interactive elements whose overall pattern and underlying dynamic can be profoundly illuminated by a magic square analysis. Just as you learned to interpret your personal characteristics in Chapter 1, you can gain an understanding of how your personality and your partner's are likely to interact at the level of cosmic energies. Then you'll be able to make a creative and personalized interpretation based on what you each know about each other.

MEASURING COMPATIBILITY

Compatibility can be assessed in a variety of degrees, based on the way your energies interact in the three different categories of personality represented by the three numbers:

- Comparing your year numbers will show how you and your partner are likely to relate at a deep level, over long periods of time and in relation to major life events.
- Comparing your month numbers will indicate how you relate at the level of communication and emotion.
- Comparing your outer numbers illuminates your ability to work together and do things together on a day-to-day basis.

Within these categories, you can compare your energies at several different levels. The first level looks at compatibility in terms of the Oriental concept of yin and yang; the next level considers the interaction of the *elements* involved; and the third level examines how the specific characteristics of your magic square numbers will combine.

When traditional Chinese astrology interprets these factors, it comes up with a hard-and-fast set of combinations, rigidly classified as "auspicious" or "inauspicious." But this old-style approach is based on certain unspoken criteria, rooted in a traditional society that was extremely stable and survived for an incredibly long time. Nowadays, we are likely to look at relationships differently. We may be prepared to accept the challenges they present, with a view to making it all work better, rather than deterministically saying that this relationship simply won't work, and this other one will, with no allowance for the operation of free will and effort. Besides, even if you want to take a deterministic view, certain combinations might work in today's postfeminist industrial society that simply wouldn't have in ancient rural China.

Let's now look at these three levels of compatibility analysis in more detail.

YIN–YANG COMPATIBILITY

The first step is to get a broad view of the fundamental energies contained within your relationship. This is done by carrying out a simple yin-yang analysis on the interaction of your charts.

You will recall that the numbers 2, 5, and 8 (earth) and 6 and 7 (metal) represent the more yang, downward and contractive side of the cycle of transforming energies in the Earth's atmosphere; that numbers 9 (fire) and 3 and 4 (wood) express the more yin, upward and expansive energies; and that number 1 (water) denotes the floating or transitional state in between, as shown in Figure 4-1.

Let's take as an example the person whose chart we worked out in Chapter 2, and an imagined partner with a different chart. We'll call them Robert and Judy.

Robert 8:4:9   Judy 7:1:2

First of all, let's look at their charts individually. Robert has a yang year number, but a yin month and outer number. Judy also has a yang year number, with a neutral month

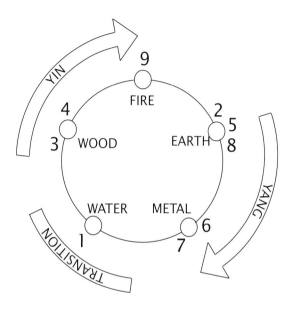

4-1. The yin and yang numbers.

number and yang outer number. In the couple's energetic "balance sheet," there's a little more yang energy than yin.

Now, let's compare the yin-yang qualities in their three personality departments. In year nature they are both on the yang side, so they will have this point in common, creating empathy. In month number, Robert is more yin than Judy, who is neutral. In more superficial aspects, Judy is more yang and Robert is more yin. These latter two variations of their basic energetic polarity will enhance their potential relationship, meaning that their energies can interact in a number of different combinations within an overall balance.

Generally speaking, a favorable energy setup includes a mixture of harmony, diversity, polarity, and balance. A situation where one person is more yang than the other in all three categories will present challenges. This is something to bear in mind as a background to the more in-depth analysis that follows.

FIVE-ELEMENT COMPATIBILITY

The next step in examining the influences at work in your relationship is to look at which elements feature in your two charts and how they interact. Each person's three-number chart will include up to three different elements. Their relationship to one another is perhaps the most powerful factor in compatibility.

To understand how these element influences interact, we must go back and look again at the cycle of Five Elements that we introduced in Chapter 1. In this circle of energies, each element has a distinctly different connection with each of the other elements, and every connection carries different implications for compatibility. The interactions of the elements follow two basic patterns, which are known as the *cycle of support* and the *cycle of control*. (There's also a third way in which the elements can relate to one another, following from these two basic cycles; we'll explore it a bit later in this chapter.)

The Cycle of Support

In the natural cycle of the seasons, each element prepares the way for the next in a progressive cycle. In deep winter's dormancy, preparations for spring are already going on below the surface, a readiness for the buds to burst forth and the bulbs to shoot up. Similarly, the growth of spring already contains the beginnings of the flower buds that will later blossom as summer approaches. The flowers contain preparations for the fruit to set, in early autumn, and the fruit contains the embryonic seeds that set in later autumn. The seeds are then ready for the renewed dormancy of next winter. Thus each stage supports the next, and each depends upon the preparations made in the previous stage.

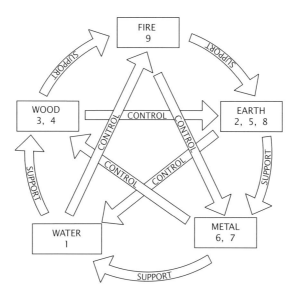

4-2. The numbers and elements: support and control cycles.

Let's translate this into the terms of the classical Five Elements, as shown in Figure 4-2:

WATER provides the essential element for wood to grow
WOOD provides the fuel for fire to burn
FIRE provides ash that nourishes the Earth
EARTH provides the ore that makes metal
METAL melts into the fluid state of water

And so each element is supported by the one preceding it, and supports the one following it, in the ongoing cycle of transformation. We'll look at what this means for relationship in a moment.

The Cycle of Control

This cycle is the other side of the coin, representing the other balancing tendency in nature. Certain energies limit or oppose others, so that nature's cycle of birth, death, and rebirth continues and the energies of the cosmos maintain a state of dynamic balance, rather than endlessly increasing. Just as the forces of yin and yang both complement and counteract each other, each element has a relationship of inhibition with another two, balancing its supporting relationship with the two remaining. So each element limits one other, and is limited by yet another; these are the two elements that are found on the opposite side of the circle. Control, like support, proceeds in an ever-continuing cycle, maintaining the balance and making each element equally important, equally powerful, and equally integrated into the whole elegant pattern. So:

WATER can extinguish fire
FIRE can melt metal
METAL can cut wood
WOOD can penetrate earth, as do the roots of trees and plants
EARTH can contain water, as in the banks of rivers and lakes

These relationships produce the classic star-shaped pattern imposed on the circular pattern of the support cycle, as we see in Figure 4-2. This control cycle has an effect on the way two people relate to one another that is just as powerful as that of the cycle of support.

Applying the Five-Element Analysis

Now you can compare your elements with those of your partner, in the three departments—deeper nature, communicative nature, and surface nature. Of these, the elemental comparison of your deeper nature—your two year numbers—is traditionally regarded as the most powerful influence on the dynamics of the relationship.

In each category in your chart, the other person's number will have one of the following relationships to yours:

- The same element
- The supporting element
- The supported element
- The controlling element
- The controlled element

When your two elements share a supporting connection, this is traditionally considered a good basis for a harmonious relationship. There is a measure of polarity, which creates attraction, but enough affinity to make for ease of communication and empathy.

If your two elements have a controlling connection, this is traditionally considered less harmonious, but it adds a component of attraction—the pull of elemental opposites. There may be excitement and variety galore in such a relationship, but communication, goal sharing, and understanding may not be easy.

If you share the same element, you will probably have a great deal in common and feel great empathy for one another, but because there's no polarity, there may not be such a strong "spark." This combination usually has a very stable quality—perhaps too stable. This is traditionally reckoned to indicate moderate compatibility.

How do you use this information? First of all, look at which elements are present in the total combination of your two charts. Then, look at your respective elements in each chart position—who's supporting whom and who's controlling whom. Finally, you can bring the whole picture together and draw some conclusions. Here's an example.

SAMPLE FIVE-ELEMENT ANALYSIS

Let's look again at the case we've already analyzed in terms of yin and yang balance, Robert and Judy. This pair's combination of charts incorporates every single element—with earth occurring twice—which indicates a healthy breadth of energies and expression in the relationship as a whole. Many relationships have a smaller range of elements or one element predominating, which will tend to narrow the range of energies and expression. Earth and metal, the year elements, will be the most prominent in Robert and Judy's relationship's energies.

Let's look more closely at the elemental relationships in each category (Figure 4–3). In year number, Robert's earth supports Judy's metal. In month number, Judy's water supports Robert's wood. In outer number, Robert's fire supports Judy's earth.

Overall, this relationship shows a high degree of classic compatibility, for all three categories involve a support connection. Judy receives the greater part of the flow of support energies, but both parties benefit from the compatibility in each of the three categories.

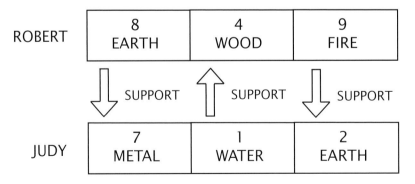

4-3. Five-Element analysis of a sample couple.

NINE-NUMBER COMPATIBILITY

The final step in measuring compatibility is to look at how the specific influences of the nine personality types interact within your relationship. At this level of analysis, traditional Chinese astrology has strongly held ideas about which numbers are most compatible, especially in year number combinations. There is certainly a sound basis for these conventional views, but they should be interpreted with discrimination rather than regarded as carved in stone.

For this step, we need to look again at the magic square. The influence we're looking at here is discovered through the respective positions in the square occupied by the numbers in each of the three personality cat-

egories, considered alongside the very powerful influence of the element combinations we have just examined (Figure 4-4).

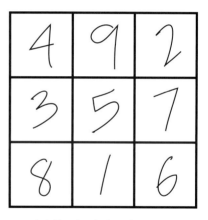

Let's look first at year numbers, whose connection means most for your compatibility. There are two ways to find the numbers that are traditionally considered most compatible with yours. First, there are the numbers that are directly connected to yours in the cycle of supporting elements, either supporting yours or supported by it. Second, there is the number that is directly opposite yours on the standard magic square (Figure 4-5). As we discussed in Chapter

4-4. The standard magic square.

2, these opposites are conventionally regarded as the most powerfully attracting numbers, and their energetic connection can override or mask the limiting influence of the control cycle. In one of the mystical properties of numbers, you can easily work out the *attracting* number that corresponds to yours by simply subtracting your own

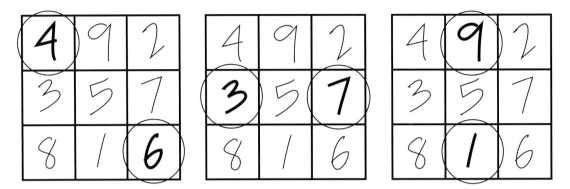

4-5. Examples of attracting numbers, directly opposite each other in the standard magic square.

year number from 10. Attracting numbers are used only in considering year number combinations, the most profound indicator of compatibility.

The pairing of attracting numbers creates the strongest pull of all between human beings, and it is found at the heart of many celebrated romances, such as John and Jackie Kennedy and John Lennon and Yoko Ono. However, this is merely an energy that pulls two people toward one another; it is not enough on its own to make a relationship work. It generally takes elements of harmony and communication in the astrological combination as well—plus working at it!

Figure 4-6 sums up the number combinations that are most attracting, moderately compatible, and least compatible. The numbers considered moderately compatible with yours are those that are the same number or the same element as yours—unless the latter happens to be your attracting number, lying opposite on the magic square. The numbers traditionally reckoned to be least compatible with yours are those that are connected in the control cycle—unless one happens to be your attracting number.

The number combinations that occur in the other two chart positions represent less fundamental indicators of compatibility, but still have important bearing on your

ELEMENT	NUMBER	ATTRACTING NUMBER	MODERATELY COMPATIBLE	LESS COMPATIBLE
WATER	1	9	1	–
EARTH	2	8	2 5	1
WOOD	3	7	3 4	258
WOOD	4	6	3 4	258
EARTH	5	5	2 8	1
METAL	6	4	6 7	9
METAL	7	3	6 7	9
EARTH	8	2	5 8	1
FIRE	9	1	9	–

4-6. Table of number compatibility.

relationship. Having the same month number, for instance, can be an extremely powerful enhancement, as it makes for profound communication and mutual understanding. Sharing the same outer number can be a modest benefit, because it indicates similar habits and outward traits. Each of these can play an important role, but won't override challenging year number factors.

The Family Roles of the Nine Numbers

There's one further way to interpret these number pairings. Each number carries an archetypal "family" role, which is assigned to these numbers in traditional Chinese cosmology. So you can gain additional understanding of the interaction of your year number with your partner's by bringing together your two *family archetypes:*

1 = Middle son
2 = Mother
3 = Eldest son
4 = Eldest daughter
5 = Seventh child
6 = Father
7 = Youngest daughter
8 = Youngest son
9 = Middle daughter

For example, in the relationship we've been looking at, Robert's number 8 is associated with the youngest son, while Judy's number 7 represents the youngest daughter. So even as they grow old, this couple will always have something of the dynamic of the young brother and sister. For instance, they will be able to benefit from others' experiences, learn from other people who have pioneered in a field of progress, enjoy being taken care of—and enjoy having this in common with one another.

CASE STUDY: PRINCE CHARLES AND PRINCESS DIANA

Let's now apply this whole process of compatibility testing to a well-known relationship. Charles was born on November 14, 1948, so his numbers are 7:8:4 (metal/earth/wood). Diana was born on July 1, 1961; her numbers were 3:1:7 (wood/water/metal).

Now let's compare these numbers within each of the three chart positions. If you look back to Figure 4-2, you'll see the most striking feature of this pair's combined chart: they had no elements in common and no supporting element combinations, only inhibiting or control dynamics.

In terms of overall yin-yang analysis, Charles' makeup is more predominantly yang, grounded and inwardly turned. Diana's chart has more yin energies, making for lightness and outgoingness.

Looking at their three personality categories individually, we see that in terms of both year (or deeper) and month (or communicative) nature, Charles had the controlling energies, whereas in the realm of outward appearances and immediate effects, Diana had the upper hand. Anyone in Diana's position might understandably have suffered from this degree of control in the two more fundamental life categories. She might also have been tempted to use her power in the third category to try to redress the balance— for instance, by rather hasty outpourings in TV interviews. At least she could get some benefit from this; when Charles did the same, it wasn't so successful an exercise. When they battled in the realm of the outer numbers, Diana was sure to win.

In their relationship, there was clearly a great attraction of opposites. In fact, they had attracting year numbers—in this case 7 and 3. Sadly, it seems that this attraction did not make up for the lack of shared aspects or supporting energies. In terms of *family archetype* numbers, Diana was the eldest son, while Charles is the youngest daughter, which may go some way toward explaining how Diana could often *seem* to be the one with the more dominant persona.

Remember, astrological compatibility isn't about whether certain relationships are "good" or "bad." When combinations of energies are naturally harmonious, you can take advantage of them. When they aren't, you can use astrological analysis to better understand the nature of the conflicting energies that need to be recognized, addressed, and assimilated—and then do something about it. Besides, even the most stable and harmonious relationship contains conflict, and that isn't a bad thing—in fact, it's probably essential. The trick is to understand the nature of such interacting energies in order to understand what you're dealing with; then you can take steps to make things work better. And that's what the following section is all about.

WORKING WITH YOUR RELATIONSHIP POTENTIAL

So now you've thoroughly checked out the prospects for any relationship. As you've seen, some combinations offer more straightforward compatibility than others, but even the least fortuitous combination is workable—and even the most fortunate will not work without effort. Of course, all relationships require certain basic inputs, such as commitment, communication, desire, expression of affection or respect, preservation of personal identity, and sheer investment of time and effort. But some of these inputs will prove particularly crucial in certain combinations and some in others. And some will mean harder work than others, depending on the energies involved.

Broadly speaking, the classically less compatible relationships, characterized by strongly antagonistic energies, will require strong and constant efforts to bridge the gaps, while the more placid combinations of kindred spirits will need to work at avoiding blandness. The more ideal combinations that lie between these extremes may well require a mixture of both strategies. A great deal of what it takes to make a relationship work is common sense, but sudoku astrology can add direction and specific guidance, using the subtle interactions of the Five Elements and the nine influences to maximize the potential and minimize the shortcomings of any pair. There's no need for you to end up as one of those torn-apart couples who helplessly bleat, "It was never meant to be!"

First of all, it's fruitful to consider the steps you can take personally to deal with the tendencies inherent in your nature, especially those qualities that will most directly affect your prospects in romance and other relationships—whoever you're with. Then you can go on to explore measures that will improve the prospects in particular relationships, first in terms of element combinations and then in interactions of the nine types.

Developing Your Own Potential

The first factor in any relationship with another person is your relationship with yourself. Clichéd, perhaps—but true. If you're happy and fulfilled in yourself, then you're obviously going to be an easier person to be in a relationship with; you're going to choose partners more wisely; and you're likely to be better at getting a relationship to succeed. Sudoku astrology offers a special opportunity to give structure to this inner work by helping you balance your own energies, with emphasis on the qualities that will most profoundly affect your interaction with another human being.

The first thing to do is to look again at the inherent qualities of your year number, and then think about those that may have a detrimental effect on your relationship and what you might be able to do about it. For instance, if you are aware of a tendency to worry too much about small matters, you might make sure that you talk matters through with your partner so that you can keep things in perspective. Here's a brief summary of the potential qualities of each type that may present challenges in how you relate to others. You can go back to Chapters 2 and 3 for more detail.

Year Number 1★
- Insecure
- Easily swayed
- Worries unnecessarily
- Doesn't want to cause any trouble
- Doesn't always show what he or she is feeling

★See Figure 2-1 to find your year number.

Year Number 2

- Conservative tendency
- Can be reticent
- Sometimes self-sacrificing
- Stronger on ideals and aspirations than on seeing things through

Year Number 3

- Ambitious
- Independent
- Can be rash or hasty
- Sensitive, may be easily hurt
- Unpredictable and quick to change
- Sometimes overwhelmingly enthusiastic or brutally frank

Year Number 4

- Tends to act on impulse
- Changeable and indecisive
- Turbulent emotions
- Confusion, lack of clarity or single-mindedness
- Can be taken in by the unscrupulous

Year Number 5

- Given to extremes
- Can be tactless
- Needs to be the center of attention
- May be controlling, manipulative, or inconsiderate
- Not strong on expressing emotional needs

Year Number 6
- Stubborn
- Cool or reserved
- Can be calculating
- Focuses strongly on self
- Likes to dominate a relationship
- Rigidity, pride, and inflexible will

Year Number 7
- Can be hedonistic
- Self-interested
- May be arrogant
- Can easily feel constrained
- Moods may oscillate widely
- Nervousness about commitment

Year Number 8
- Can be stubborn
- Resistant to change
- Prone to isolation
- Excessively high self-esteem or ego
- Can be hard to get to know
- May be haughty, aloof, or distant-seeming

Year Number 9
- Impatient
- Lack of self-control

- Can be inconstant
- May be fickle or vain
- Trouble with long-term commitment
- Easily influenced by stronger individuals

In the interest of balanced and harmonious relationships, it is also worthwhile to explore the balance and harmony of your own life in terms of the Five Elements. First, make sure that you are truly expressing your native element. If your year number is 9, for instance, make sure that you're living your fire nature in your activities, career, hobbies, and so on, rather than suppressing it. If you need to refresh your memory, you can look back to the descriptions of elemental qualities in Chapter 2 and pick up some pointers.

Second, acquaint yourself with the two elements that naturally complement yours—those that lie on either side of yours on the Five-Element support cycle. Make sure that you are capable, in your life, of overlapping into their territory—living the qualities they represent—for this is a natural part of your inherent potential. Here's a recap of the supporting and supported elements that each type would do well to incorporate:

FIRE PERSON: Include wood and earth patterns
EARTH PERSON: Include metal and fire patterns
METAL PERSON: Include water and earth patterns
WATER PERSON: Include wood and metal patterns
WOOD PERSON: Include fire and water patterns

Third, pay attention to the qualities associated with the elements that relate to yours on the control cycle. Broadly speaking, the challenging personality aspects we've described, which signify the low end of your potential for self-expression and relating, correspond to qualities associated with these two elements on the far side of the circle from yours—the positive qualities that you are missing.

Finally, consider your three-number makeup; this little matrix is, in essence, a summary of your relationship with yourself. We've already discussed how to interpret it as an indicator of the total person; if you can manage to integrate its diverse aspects fully within yourself, including any conflicting elemental energies they contain, then your potential for relationships will be that much better. Understanding and expressing your true self, and having the flexibility and adaptability to let another person do the same, is the bottom line—the key to success in any relationship.

Developing Your Partnership

As you've seen in the first part of this chapter, the interaction of your year element and your partner's is probably the strongest single factor in overall compatibility. It plays a major part in determining how your sexuality, emotions, and basic way of being are likely to interact with your partner's—and traditional thinking rates some combinations a lot more highly than others in terms of conventional workability. However, there *are* things you can do to improve the potential of any element combination. Let's look at the possibilities.

COPING WITH CONFLICTING ELEMENTS

When your year numbers have elements that relate to each other on the control cycle, such as metal and fire or water and earth, you're facing the most challenging relationship situation. As we've seen, there is an inherent opposition of energies and lack of empathy between the elements. Obviously, all relationships have their conflicts and their ups and downs, and this is as it should be. It's just that in relationships between conflicting elements, the ups and downs are going to be a more dramatic and frequent feature of the landscape. In such a relationship it will take longer to establish stability and build up trust. In the long run, though, facing and surviving these difficulties together may create its own strong bond.

To make a success of a controlling combination, it is important to create the missing relationship dynamics of support and harmony in other ways. These could include:

- Keeping channels of communication open
- Making a special effort to do things together
- Going in for activities that your partner enjoys, even if they're not your favorites
- Being particularly tolerant of your partner's outlook on life where it differs from yours
- Being prepared to compromise in your actions while preserving your own identity
- Trying to really understand what is going on in your partner's mind and heart
- Letting your partner know what *you're* thinking and feeling
- Finding ways to nurture one another
- Being sensitive to your partner's sexual needs and preferences
- Keeping in touch when you're apart

It's also important to take note of the *direction* of control in the Five-Element dynamics and take steps to balance out the natural tendency for one of you to consistently dominate or constrain the other. For example, metal will tend to cut back on the freedom of wood, and earth will tend to restrict water. Take care that one of you doesn't always wield the power, take the initiative, or inhibit the other person's freedom.

USING THE MEDIATING ELEMENTS

Another approach that can work in this type of relationship—in addition to cultivating qualities and behaviors of support—is to reintroduce the specific energies that are missing in your particular combination of opposing elements. And here sudoku astrology has a very cunning trick up its sleeve.

If a couple does not share the same element, you have learned ways that their elements can relate to one another on the support cycle or on the control cycle and how to use these. However, there is a third cycle of relationship among elements, and it

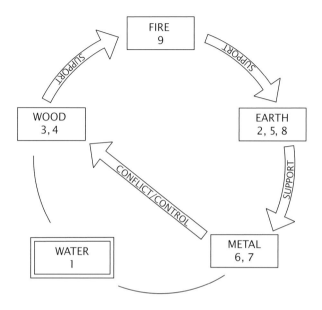

4-7. Example of mediating elements: Water mediates the conflict between metal and wood.

can play a key role in the improvement of relationship potential. This is known as the *mediating cycle,* illustrated in Figure 4-7.

As you now know, the elements are traditionally arranged around the circle in order of supporting relationships, with relationships across the circle forming a star-shaped sequence of control. Looking at the control sequence, you can see that each element bypasses the element that is adjacent to it on the circle and controls the one that is next in the circular sequence. The bypassed element has a special potential for moderating or mitigating the conflict between the elements on either side of it. Thus each element has a mitigating relationship with two others, and these combinations create the *mediating cycle:*

FIRE mediates the conflict between wood and earth
EARTH mediates the conflict between fire and metal
METAL mediates the conflict between earth and water
WATER mediates the conflict between metal and wood
WOOD mediates the conflict between water and fire

So the trick is to bring into your situation the energies of the element that has this mitigating effect on your conflict of elements. If you and your partner have a combination of metal and wood, for instance, you would seek ways of bringing in the positive qualities of water—for instance, being flexible toward each other's ideas rather than having to have your own way, or relaxing and going with the flow more often. You could even avail yourself of the actual physical presence of water energy, by spending time near water or having a water feature in your garden or home.

CULTIVATING SUPPORTING ELEMENTS

If your year elements are connected by the cycle of support, you already have the makings of a naturally more stable and straightforward relationship. No doubt you'll have ups and downs, but they will not be so extreme or abrupt. There's a downside to this stability: You have a modest degree of polarity in your combination, but not quite the same dynamic attraction of opposites as in the conflicting combinations (unless you happen to have attracting numbers). So you may want to take steps to add excitement and variety to your intimacy and lovemaking, and to your whole life together.

There is also a tendency for the support cycle to have a one-sided effect: One person may be giving most of the support and the other receiving most of it. It's important to make an effort to share these roles so you don't create a situation in which one of you always leads and the other always follows, or one is completely dependent and the other feels martyred. To avoid this, the person with the supporting element can cultivate the habit of taking the lead more, and the one with the supported element can practice playing a secondary role at times. Think of these practices as a kind of role-playing: you're not denying your own basic nature, but trying on different energies from time to time.

ENHANCING SHARED ELEMENTS

Relationships in which partners share the same element are classically regarded as moderately compatible, with plenty of familiarity but little spark. The ups and downs in these relationships may be so few and so small that life can get just a bit too cozy and comfortable, or even dull; you know each other only too well. Yet there is a tendency for each partner to fail to see the other's negative aspects, and even to reinforce these qualities, so that both can descend into a deeper and deeper rut. So, to prevent either one of you from being tempted to seek excitement in a more sparky combination somewhere else, it's vital to make the most of whatever polarity does exist in your situation. This might arise from your respective month or outer numbers, but if not, you might find polarity in your social or ethnic backgrounds, family values and upbringing, and so on. You can take some common-sense measures: Define boundaries within the relationship rather than living in each other's pockets; make sure you have interests and activities outside the relationship; take separate vacations sometimes; and so on. All these things will increase polarity and therefore attraction.

But you also need to go out of your way to introduce the qualities and activities that relate to the other elements—in particular, those that are adjacent to yours on the support cycle. Thus, for example, a water couple could get into the energies of wood—doing activities that are particularly uplifting, such as going to see an inspirational movie, or one in which there is dynamic movement and action (say, white-water rafting). You could also benefit from the energies of metal, perhaps by being more forceful, organized, and focused, and applying yourselves determinedly to particular projects. You both need to go beyond your normal, safe range of activities and ways of being. In intimacy and lovemaking, you need to play games, create excitement, and introduce mystery so as not to take each other for granted.

You can also draw on the energies of close friends or family members who you know belong to other elements, either by asking their advice on relationship matters or by joining them in social activities, where their companionship and influence can enhance your own situation.

Here's a summary of elemental influences to introduce into single-element combinations:

WATER + WATER: metal, wood
WOOD + WOOD: water, fire
FIRE + FIRE: wood, earth
EARTH + EARTH: fire, metal
METAL + METAL: water, fire

USING THE MONTH AND OUTER NUMBERS

While the combination of year numbers tends to be the most powerful single influence in a relationship, you can maximize the possibilities in any pairing by extending the processes we've just explored to the rest of your combined charts.

In the first part of this chapter, you looked at your two sets of numbers and compared them in each of the three personality categories. Now it's time to determine an approach that will help make the most of the potential at every level. For instance, you may have controlling elements in your year numbers, but supporting or shared elements in your month numbers, which greatly eases conflicting energies in the relationship. You can give further emphasis to this factor by relating carefully at communicative and emotional levels, and giving importance to this kind of care within the relationship. Then this aspect of your chemistry will play a greater part in the bigger picture.

Or perhaps you have more harmonious elements in your outer numbers. Although a less powerful influence, the outer number can still be played up if you accentuate its part in your lives together by recognizing and embracing each other's habits and ways of going about daily life.

Indeed, combinations in which opposing year elements are balanced by more compatible dynamics in the other categories can form the basis of very workable relationships. The real challenge comes when there is conflict in all three categories. To get this combination to work for a whole lifetime, you'll probably have to be extremely accommodating, extremely tolerant, and extremely determined to make it work. If you're committed, it can surely be done!

There's one further strategy that you can use to get your relationship to work better, and that is to take advantage of how the dynamics of your interaction with each other vary over the course of time. And that is what you shall discover in the next chapter.

The Magic Square over Time

N ow you know a good deal about your own astrological makeup; you've gained insight into other people's nature; and you've examined the astrological dynamics of some relationships. But these aren't fixed quantities. Time does not stand still, and everything is subject to changing influences over the passage of time. All astrological systems take this into account in some way.

In many ways, sudoku astrology is simpler than zodiac astrology. One of the most elegant aspects is that the same system that gives you information about yourself—the magic square—also enables you to plot the important changing influences on your potential destiny. There's no need to work out complicated charts of the heavens at crucial moments in time. Simply by understanding the influences that change in predictable patterns, you will be better able to understand what is going on in any situation; you will be able to maximize your potential. You may come to understand better what you've experienced in the past. And you'll learn how to choose the best timing for important decisions and actions.

The way the astrological influences work over time is like this: Each year in the nine-year cycle, as you know, has a different number, and this is what gave you your year number. Each year in the cycle also has its own square, with a different configuration of numbers, and with the number of that year in the center. Depending on your *own* year number, each passing year in the cycle puts you in a different house, subject to a different influence; the squares are the maps by which you can work out influences on you in any year. Every nine years you complete a cycle; you are always born into the house of 5, for reasons you'll shortly see, and every 9 years you enter it again, with the potential for a fresh start in your life. This is why Oriental societies traditionally consider that the ages of 9, 18, 27, 36, and so on mark important phases in life.

But the influences don't just apply to years; there is also a cycle of nine months, exerting a different kind of influence. The yearly cycle has the most profound and far-reaching effects, while the monthly effects are more immediate and short lived. There's even a cycle of hours—times of day when people of different types reach their peak of energy and potential. We'll look at this last point at the end of the chapter.

In this chapter, then, you will first find out how to work out your astrological position or house for any year or month. Then you'll discover the classical interpretation for each of these houses—the kind of experience it brings, the strengths and weaknesses it highlights, the ways you are likely to react to other people, what will work well for you and what won't work so well, and so on. Lastly, you'll get pointers and strategies for working with this information so as to make life work for *you* to realize your fullest potential.

THE NINE HOUSES

Whether you're considering years or months, the magic square influences change in a continuously repeating cycle of nine, with one of the numbers dominant in each. (The dominant number in any square is the one that becomes your year or month number if you're born in that year or that month.) This sequence is represented graphically by a set of nine squares, as shown in Figure 5-1, the same ones you used in Chapter 2 to

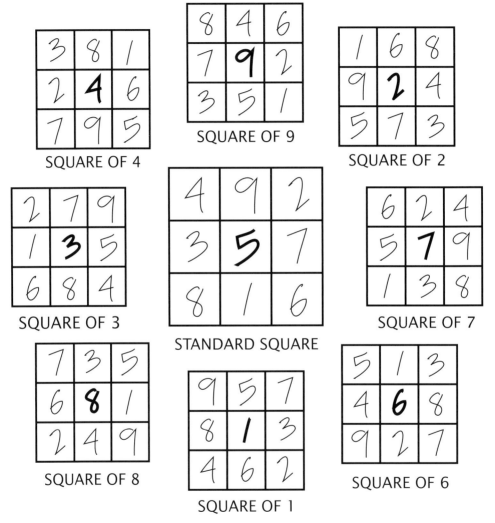

5-1. The nine sudoku astrology houses.

discover your outer number from the other two. All the numbers move into different positions as the square changes over time.

The standard square is the one that has 5 in the center, marking the midpoint of the cycle of nine years or months. This square holds the key to interpreting all the other squares and the effects of the changes of influence over time. In the standard square, all the numbers are in their "home" places, which represent all the qualities you have learned to associate with each number. These home positions, or houses, are referred to by the numbers that occupy them in the standard square. The top left position, for instance, is known as the house of 4, and the bottom middle position is the house of 1.

As time passes, you occupy the houses sequentially, which dictates the influences that you are subject to. To ascertain the influences on you in any month or year, you look at the square that applies to it, and check which position your own year number occupies in that square; then you look to the standard square to see which house this is and read the corresponding interpretation. We'll remind ourselves how to work out the correct square for any month or year in a moment.

Let's put this into practice, using the sample couple from the previous chapter. Their year numbers are:

Robert: 8   Judy: 7

When looking at the square of a given year or month, Robert will always be looking for the position occupied by the number 8. In a year or month governed by the number 1, for instance (the square with 1 at the center), 8 is in the left middle position, which in the standard square is the house of 3 (Figure 5-2). Robert will therefore be experiencing the influence of the number 3 in that year or month.

In that same year or month, Judy will be in the house of 2, because number 7 occupies the top right position in the square of 1, which is the number 2 position in the standard square (Figure 5-3).

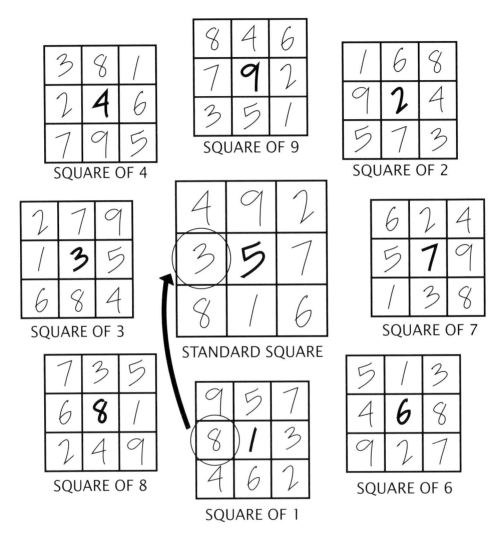

SQUARE OF 9

SQUARE OF 4

SQUARE OF 2

SQUARE OF 3

STANDARD SQUARE

SQUARE OF 7

SQUARE OF 8

SQUARE OF 1

SQUARE OF 6

5-2. In a 1 square, 8 occupies the 3 position of the standard magic square.

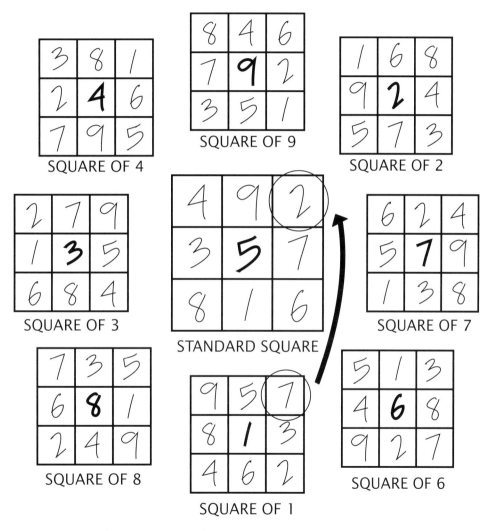

SQUARE OF 4

SQUARE OF 9

SQUARE OF 2

SQUARE OF 3

STANDARD SQUARE

SQUARE OF 7

SQUARE OF 8

SQUARE OF 1

SQUARE OF 6

5-3. In a 1 square, 7 occupies the 2 position of the standard magic square.

So all you need to know now, in order to discover which house you occupy in any year or month, is which square applies to that year or month—and you identify the square by figuring out the number of that year or month. You'll do this exactly the same way you worked out your own year and month numbers in Chapter 2. The steps are summarized here.

The number for any year can be calculated with this formula:

1. Add together the four digits of the year
2. If this new number is greater than 10, add its two digits together to produce a single-digit number
3. Subtract this number from 11 and you get the year number

For example, take the year 2009:

$2009 = 2 + 0 + 0 + 9 = 11$
$1 + 1 = 2$
$11 - 2 = 9$

So 2009 is a 9 year; its square is the one with 9 at the center.
Or take the year 2010:

$2010 = 2 + 0 + 1 + 0 = 21$
$2 + 1 = 3$
$11 - 3 = 8$

So 2009 is an 8 year.
Remember, the year begins on February 4, not January 1!
The squares for the years 2009 through 2018 are shown in Figure 5-4. You can easily work backward or forward from this set, because the center numbers simply fall

8	4	6
7	9	2
3	5	1

2009

7	3	5
6	8	1
2	4	9

2010

6	2	4
5	7	9
1	3	8

2011

5	1	3
4	6	8
9	2	7

2012

4	9	2
3	5	7
8	1	6

2013

3	8	1
2	4	6
7	9	5

2014

2	7	9
1	3	5
6	8	4

2015

1	6	8
9	2	4
5	7	3

2016

9	5	7
8	1	3
4	6	2

2017

8	4	6
7	9	2
3	5	1

2018

5-4. The squares for years 2009 through 2018; remember that the year begins in February.

MONTH	YEAR NUMBER		
	1 4 7	2 5 8	3 6 9
FEB 4 - MAR 5	8	2	5
MAR 6 - APR 4	7	1	4
APR 5 - MAY 5	6	9	3
MAY 6 - JUN 5	5	8	2
JUN 6 - JUL 7	4	7	1
JUL 8 - AUG 7	3	6	9
AUG 8 - SEP 7	2	5	8
SEP 8 - OCT 8	1	4	7
OCT 9 - NOV 7	9	3	6
NOV 8 - DEC 7	8	2	5
DEC 8 - JAN 5	7	1	4
JAN 6 - FEB 3	6	9	3

5-5. Use this table to find the number for any month. See pages 20 and 21 for details.

from 1 to 9 repeatedly. Since 2018 is a 9 year, you know that 2019 will be an 8 year, 2020 a 7 year, and so on.

The square for any month is the one with that month's number at the center. You can derive the number of a given month from the table in Figure 5-5, using the year number of the month you're interested in. Remember that the months do not start on the first calendar day.

The squares for the months June 2009 to September 2010 are shown in Figure 5-6. You can extend this series backward or forward, as the numbers at the center again fall from 1 to 9 repeatedly; or calculate the month numbers from the table.

In Figure 5-7, you'll find some blank squares you can fill in and label for a set of years or months in which you are particularly interested.

The Cycle of Energies

So now you can work out the house you have occupied or will occupy in any month or year, in the past or future. But what do all these houses mean?

There is a close relationship between

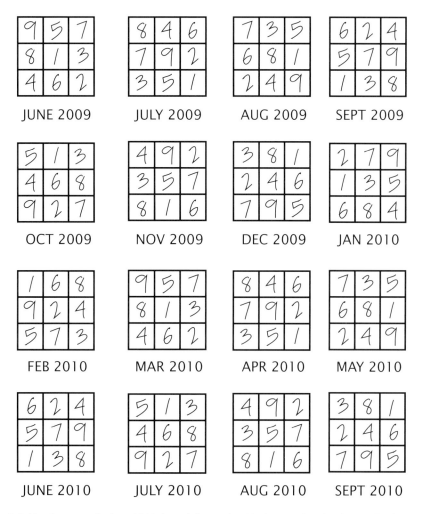

5-6. Month squares for June 2009 through September 2010; remember that the months do not begin on the first day of our Western calendar months (see Figure 2-2).

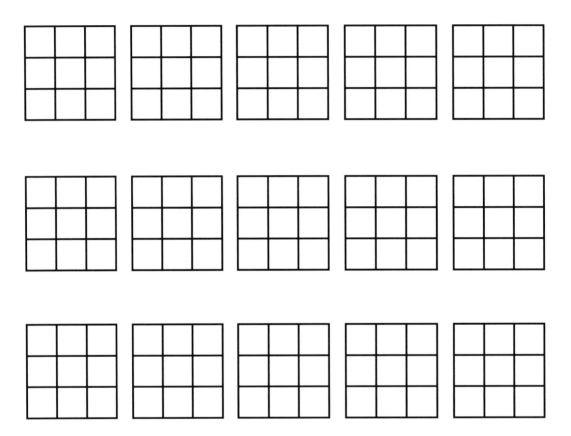

5-7. Fill in these squares with numbers to examine year and month sequences that are important for you.

the experience of occupying any house and the characteristics of the personality that goes with that number; after all, it's the astrological influence of that house that formed those characteristics. As you pass through a house, it's as if you explore your potential to become that type of person for a while, while still fundamentally being your own type of person. In the pages ahead, we'll look at the generic characteristics of the nine houses as they are going to influence our experience. In the descriptions below, another term is introduced for each number: this is the traditional Chinese image representing the way this number operates as an influence in time, rather than as a personal characteristic.

You will also notice a strong underlying pattern of sequence in the houses, analogous to the cycle of the natural world and the seasons. Each house has its positive and negative potential; none is inherently "better" or "worse" than any other. They are all stages we must pass through in order to achieve progressive and profound success and fulfillment. This is an important point to bear in mind in the age of quick fix and short attention span!

In each successive year, the number at the center of the square decreases by one. But each year, the position your year number occupies *increases* by one. This means that as you pass through the nine houses, there is a sense of natural development, like the growth from a seed (represented by the number 1 house) to full maturity and blossoming in the house of 9. So making the most of your true potential in each different house not only benefits you at the time; it also builds on the progress you've made in earlier stages and contributes to the success of future stages. This applies over the cycle of months as well as the cycle of years. If you take these influences into account, you will be working *with* the energies of the cosmos and the planet rather *against* them, so everything you do will be more effective.

None of this is destiny. It's just a question of the particular tendencies or possibilities most likely to crop up at particular times. None of the influences is all positive or all negative; it's up to you to determine their implications. As you do, you'll be better able to develop your strengths, overcome your weaknesses, and choose favorable timing to take advantage of opportunities. You'll be able to take a creative and enlightened approach to cause and effect.

The House of 1

Image: Moving water
Element: Water
Influence: Darkness

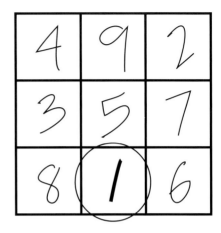

5-8. The house of 1.

The house of 1 (Figure 5-8) corresponds to the dormancy of midwinter, when some people may feel despondency or gloom—but when your number occupies this position it can be an excellent time to reflect on the past, make plans for the future, and focus on inner development, rather than putting energy into outward or social progress. You may encounter difficulty if you try to achieve too much in the tangible sense; this isn't a good time for starting new projects or taking new directions, but rather for making the inner preparations that will help new projects and directions succeed when you occupy future houses. For now, it's best to let events take their course and go with the flow of life's river. In classical Chinese parlance, this is the time for the yielding or nonstriving state. Your intuition, on the other hand, can be extremely strong and reliable at this time.

In love and relationships, you may face challenges; often they'll be caused by others rather than by you, since there's a passive quality to being in this house. Your intentions can sometimes be misunderstood; you may well lose any arguments or conflicts that you get into. If you experience a negative emotion at this time, it's likely to be fear.

You can be vulnerable and impressionable at this time, so seek the company of positive people and avoid the influence of those who are negatively inclined.

The House of 2

Image: Mother Earth
Element: Earth
Influence: Receptivity

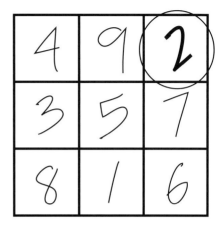

5-9. The house of 2.

You occupy the house of 2 (Figure 5-9) imme-
diately after the house of 1. This position continues the sense of slowness in outward progress
that began in the house of 1, but the outlook
begins to brighten. The ground of your life
is becoming ready for new growth, but that
growth is not as yet outwardly evident; it
won't be until you occupy the house of 3. But
the house of 2 continues to be a good time for
inner development, as well as for strengthening
friendships. It is ideal for "cleaning up your act" in preparation for the opportunities
that the following houses will bring. There may still be uncertainty in love, romance,
and relationships in general. You may tend to worry or be anxious. Try not to over-
react when you do; understand that it is inherently a passing phase. Your fluctuating
emotions may also have an upsetting effect on those close to you, so it can be helpful
to rein them in a bit. At the same time, in this phase you have greater potential than
usual for nurturing those around you.

The House of 3

Image: Thunder
Element: Wood
Influence: Proceeding

This position (Figure 5-10) represents the first tangible growth and forward movement of spring; everything seems a lot brighter, and your energies are more strongly active. It's a terrific time to start a project or venture, to pursue your ambitions, and to advance toward your goals. At this time it's appropriate to act quickly, seize opportunities assertively, and proceed steadily but energetically.

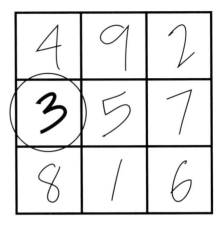

5-10. The house of 3.

Of course, these strong energies may have a downside. Difficult emotions that can surface in this house are impatience, frustration, and anger—particularly if you come up against people or things that seem to block your progress.

Love and relationships offer more dynamic prospects in your life in this house, whether for the year or for the month; a new relationship may start, or an existing one may be renewed and revitalized. It's a good time for you to take the lead in exploring new activities and trying new variations on your old patterns. If you've become stuck in any kind of rut, this is the perfect time to shift things forward. But remember that other people around you may not be feeling quite so dynamic. Take this into account in your exciting plans, and take care to appreciate others fully—even if it's not what comes naturally to you at this time.

The House of 4

Image: The Wind
Element: Wood
Influence: Preparation

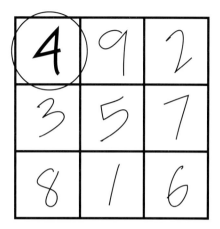

5-11. The house of 4.

This is where the first energies of early spring disperse and lose the quality of a single, unstoppable direction, manifesting instead as the more diffuse energy of later spring (Figure 5-11). The outlook is still bright, but the forward progress initiated in the previous house is less dramatic. Continuing with the processes you started in the house of 3 will generally be more fruitful than launching brand-new activities and ventures or moving in completely new directions.

The sense of dispersing energies makes itself felt like a changeable wind that can come from any direction and blow hard or soft. So it's helpful to have a plan in mind for everything you do, in order to keep your forward momentum and avoid dissipating your creative energies. It's particularly important to avoid being hasty or impulsive. As with the previous house—also governed by the wood element—you may find yourself responding to hindrance with frustration or impatience, or even with anger.

Relationships already under way can benefit greatly at this time, continuing to develop and grow, with ever deeper trust and harmony. Even as you enjoy this advantage, you'll need to keep an open mind, take special care to be aware of other people's needs, and be careful not to set your emotional ideals too high.

This house marks the end of the yin, upward energy cycle, before energy settles into the house of 5.

The House of 5

Image: The Center
Element: Earth
Influence: Fluctuation

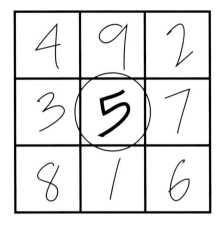

5-12. The house of 5.

This house (Figure 5-12) places you at the ultimate point of balance—between yin and yang forces, between the upward-growing and the inward-settling energies, between the poles of heaven and earth. It carries the sense of being at the center of things, where everything tends to move toward you without your needing to shift. The house of 5 is, in fact, the house that you were born into, because in the square of your birth year, your year number always occupies the central position. And you enter this house again after two nine-year cycles, when you are eighteen—a pivotal time, poised between childhood and adulthood. In many countries it's the age when you can vote, buy alcohol, and take on other rights and responsibilities of adult life. It's traditionally associated with the situation of the king or emperor—that is, the person in control.

In the sequence of the nine houses, this is also a point of change from upward growth to inward consolidation. At this pivotal time, actions you take have more power invested in them, and therefore greater effect, for better or for worse. The experience of being in this house can draw you to extremes, both positive and negative. You are likely to have bigger ups and downs, but at the same time you'll probably find yourself better equipped than usual to deal with them. It is a time to take care, to be cautious, to stay within the limits of your ability and be open to input and advice from others. You'll find yourself wanting to be the center of attention and of other people's activities, but try not to let this tendency get out of hand. Whatever flexibility you can muster will help a great deal.

In relationships, too, you may be exposed to extremes of positive and negative, including the reappearance of circumstances and patterns that you thought belonged strictly to the past. People close to you may also experience these strong effects through you, because your influence is so powerful when in this house; they may even begin to perceive you as split into two quite different personalities or ways of being. So take care to talk things through with others and to listen to what they have to say.

The House of 6

Image: Heaven

Element: Metal

Influence: Prosperity

This position (Figure 5-13) relates to the time of early autumn and the harvest, when you reap the benefits of the efforts you've made in the previous five stages. It is a stage in which enterprises can more easily bring rewards; it is traditionally regarded as a materially favorable and fortunate house.

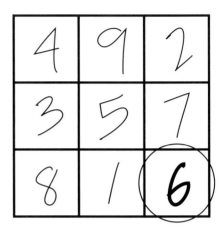

5-13. The house of 6.

It's also a good time to enjoy life, to celebrate, and to follow desires. In contrast, it's important to guard against overconfidence or arrogance at this time, and you will be wise to listen to the advice of others. Likewise, the fruits of success—whether physical, material, emotional, or sexual—need to be managed appropriately and not squandered, just as the grain from the harvest has to be stored and measured out, in order to last until the next autumn.

And it's a time when you can deepen your own personal resources—your wisdom and maturity, your sense of responsibility, your capacity to meet life's demands when less fortunate times come.

Similarly, your relationships can gain strength, deepen, and stabilize. People close to you may instinctively recognize the strength and authority of your position at this time, and they may support you in the steps you take to improve the status quo. Yet it's worth saying again—don't let this go to your head, or think you always know what's best for everyone else. Don't believe your own PR!

The House of 7

Image: Harvest
Element: Metal
Influence: Joy

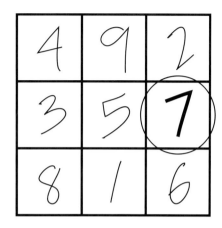

5-14. The house of 7.

This is the phase of later autumn, when energies settle still further (Figure 5-14). There is celebration that the harvest is gathered in and that you are enjoying the fruits of earlier efforts. Life has a quality of smoothness and ease. A more mellow type of satisfaction arises, materially, mentally, and emotionally.

You will do best, therefore, to be fairly conservative—to maintain the activities, patterns, and approaches that are already working for you. Stick to what you know, rather than stepping out into the unfamiliar. Your inner maturity can continue to develop here, with the benefit of self-reflection, and often with a spiritual dimension or a deepening insight into life. You also have a strong ability to inspire others.

In terms of intimate relationships, there is a stronger than usual attraction to the opposite sex, but new encounters at this time may not be profound or long-lasting. Affairs at this time are likely to produce unhappiness all round. You'll also need to watch out for a tendency to jealousy. When things aren't going so well, the negative emotions that you are likely to feel most strongly in this house are sadness and depression. Take care not to become too introspective or isolated; communication within relationships is particularly important.

The House of 8

Image: The Mountain

Element: Earth

Influence: Stillness

This is a time of drawing in energies into the stillness of the mountain, which also offers the prospect of farsighted perspective (Figure 5-15). It's a time of the turning of energies, too, before the dramatic experience of being in the 9 house. Often associated with revolution, it is a time when many things in your life can change, including your way of thinking.

Correspondingly, it's an excellent opportunity to review yourself and your whole situation, and perhaps consider what parts are worth keeping and what can be let go. With this capacity for farsighted vision, it is also wise to beware of egocentricity, aloofness, stubbornness, or inflexible points of view.

In relationships, this can be a great time to clear up outstanding items on your agenda or resolve issues left over from the past that may be causing frustration. This can greatly brighten the future. People around you may well have difficulty knowing what's going on with your emotions, for you may be more vulnerable, yet less revealing, than usual. Jealousy or guilt could rear its ugly head at this time. So make sure to express clearly what's going on for you and what you want from any relationship.

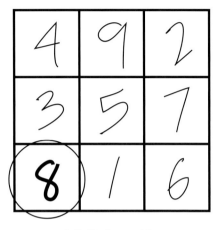

5-15. The house of 8.

The House of 9

Image: Flickering Fire
Element: Fire
Influence: Brightness

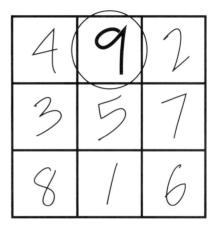

5-16. The house of 9.

This is the time of full maturity, illumination, and clarity, when the nine-house cycle reaches its peak of fulfillment, like the bright blossoming of flowers in the summer (Figure 5-16). It's an extremely active time, when you'll find you're able to do most of what you want to do. You'll have lots of new ideas, along with opportunities to realize long-held dreams or ambitions—especially if you've already taken the opportunities in the other houses to lay the groundwork. However, it's wise at this time to be wary of extremes, and to be orderly and organized in your way of going about life, in order to minimize the chaotic potential this house can have.

Relations with others can be very positive. Love and romance can flourish; encounters may be plentiful but not necessarily deep. You can make many new friends, but may lose some old ones. In any existing long-term relationship, you may need to keep your whirlwind emotions from having a disturbing effect on your partner. It may also be difficult for others close to you to keep up with the high levels of your energy and personal evolution, which can prove upsetting for them and frustrating for you. Be aware that others around you may be more grounded than you, and take advantage of their stability.

Lots of things about you may well become known to others at this time—some of which you may not be pleased to have exposed. So if you've been covering something up, it may be better to come clean than to be found out!

And even as you're enjoying the brilliant energy of 9, you're also paving the way for reentering the house of 1 and starting the cycle all over again.

WHAT THE HOUSES MEAN FOR YOU

Although you may know the overall characteristics of the different houses, there are a number of factors to bear in mind when using them to illuminate your own fortunes. You'll want to know how the houses affect people of different numbers and elements differently; how to apply the information in different ways to years and to months; and how to make the most of the two houses, year and month, that you occupy at any time.

Generally speaking, when you're in a house governed by the same element as your number, or by its supporting element, you will feel more comfortable and at home. When you're in the house of a counteracting element, you'll tend to feel a little bit out of your element, and generally need to put a bit more effort into what you do. A table of year numbers, with the counteracting numbers for each, is given in Figure 5-17.

Your Year and Month Houses

The effect of being in any house is much more deep-seated and long-lasting for a year than for a month. As the house you occupy in any year is one stage of a nine-year cycle, what you can achieve and experience in that year will have repercussions throughout the rest of the nine-year period. Correspondingly, your experiences and actions in a particular month have an effect throughout a whole nine-month cycle—the gestation period, as it happens, for human beings. So the interpretation of your month house tells you more about immediate and short-term effects, and applies more to transient aspects of your being—especially emotions—while the year house signals broad shifts in the pattern of your life.

YOUR NUMBER	COUNTERACTING NUMBERS	SAME OR SUPPORTING NUMBERS
1 (WATER)	2, 5, 8, 9 (EARTH, FIRE)	1, 6, 7 (WATER, METAL)
2, 5, 8 (EARTH)	1, 3, 4 (WATER, WOOD)	2, 5, 8, 9 (EARTH, FIRE)
3, 4 (WOOD)	2, 5, 6, 7, 8 (EARTH, METAL)	1, 3, 4 (WATER, WOOD)
6, 7 (METAL)	3, 4, 9 (WOOD, FIRE)	2, 5, 6, 7, 8 (EARTH, METAL)
9 (FIRE)	1, 6, 7 (WATER, METAL)	3, 4, 9 (WOOD, FIRE)

5-17. Counteracting and supporting numbers.

It's also important to realize that you're experiencing both cycles at the same time, so the pattern of monthly effects is superimposed on the pattern of the years. This means that in a year spent in the house of 9, let's say, you'll also be passing through twelve month houses, three of them repeated. Some of these superimpositions will reinforce each other, as when you're also in the month house of 9; others will have a neutralizing effect, as when you're in the house of 1 for the month. There's a range of combination effects, too, which will become clear as we look at the ways in which people with different year numbers react in different houses.

So in practice, every single month in the whole nine-year cycle is a unique combination of year and month influences—eighty-one in all—that you can use to weave an incredibly rich and varied tapestry in the fabric of your life and relationships. So there's no excuse for complaining that things never seem to change! If you're feeling this way, you must not be taking advantage of your life's infinitely varied potential.

Using the Houses in Relationships

You've seen how the houses affect you according to your year number. You will also tend to relate differently to other people with different year numbers, according to what house you are currently occupying. When you're in the 9 house, for instance, people whose year number is 9 will seem somehow familiar and more understandable. They will seem to be your natural allies, supporters, or advisers. This is because they are permanently in tune with what you are temporarily going through. People with elements antagonistic to that of your house, however, will interact with you quite differently. A number 1 person, for instance, may seem to be your opponent, because he or she is ruled by water, and you are in the house of fire; while a 6 or 7 person, being metal, might have that impression about you (fire controls metal). None of this runs very deep; it's more a matter of superficial reactions, which can easily be overcome by reflection and clear communication.

In terms of love and romance, the phenomenon of *attracting numbers*, which we explored in Chapter 4, may be more manifest at certain times, depending on your house position for the year. You may notice that you are particularly attracted to people whose year number occupies the opposite position in the magic square to the one you're occupying at the time, even though their energies are elementally opposed to what you are currently experiencing. So when you're in that 9 house, though 9 is not your year number, you may find yourself drawn to number 1 people. The following year, when you are in the 1 house, you may suddenly be noticing only 9 people! If so, bear in mind that this is a transitory attraction, not nearly as strong a basis for a long-term relationship as one based on your birth chart and theirs. (Of course, if you just want a quick fling . . .)

If you're in an ongoing partnership, this dynamic appears in another way. You and your partner will feel a particularly strong romantic and sexual attraction when the two of you happen to be occupying opposite houses. The pairs of attracting house numbers are set out in Figure 5-18 as a reminder. In fact, the pattern of your whole relationship will be affected at some level by the interaction of the pair of houses that you are respectively occupying at any time. You can get insight into this effect by reviewing the now familiar interaction of elements and numbers (see Chapter 4).

One of the most powerful ways to make creative use of this information in a

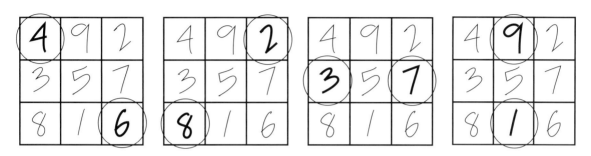

5-18. The four pairs of attracting year numbers.

relationship is to exploit the characteristics of the houses that you and your partner respectively occupy at any time. Whichever of you is in a more favorable position for certain roles, responsibilities, or activities can be in charge of those on behalf of you both. So, for instance, the person who is occupying the number 6 house can naturally do more of the decision-making and organize any celebrations, while a partner who is in number 2 house can focus on preparations for something in the future, such as moving or taking a trip. The person occupying the 8 house may be in the best position for thinking important decisions through, while someone in the 9 position could handle the couple's social calendar!

You can also maximize your combined potential by working constructively with the interaction of the elements of the houses that you each occupy. When the elements of your houses are the same, you can get to know each other better. When these elements are in a supporting relationship, such as fire and earth, you can build up the relationship's storehouse of harmony and mutual understanding. In this situation, it will be advantageous for you both if the person in the supported position, in this case earth, takes more initiative in joint matters, and the person in the supporting position (wood) does more backing up.

When the houses you occupy have antagonistic elements, you can counteract any difficulties you experience by staying in touch, working on communication, and keeping differences of opinion or conflict in perspective—and remembering that whatever you're experiencing is a phase, not forever. At the same time, you may also have the opportunity to enjoy the increased interest or attraction that can come from the polarity of your houses. Again, the person in the *controlling* position can take more initiative than the *controlled,* whose actions will tend to be dampened. All these dynamics will naturally have a greater impact in the houses of years than the houses of months and, as we've seen, the month pattern will be superimposed repeatedly on the deeper pattern of the years.

TIMES FOR SPECIAL CARE

There is one more factor—a very influential one—to take into account if you want to maximize the benefit of knowing your position in the square of any year or month. It involves three specific ways in which your number's position relates to the position of certain other numbers, combinations that traditionally call for a conservative, cautious, or even passive approach to planning and action. This factor overrides the indications given by your year house alone. Arranged from the most influential to the least influential, the combinations are as follows:

1. When your year number occupies the position directly *opposite the number 5* in the square of a year or month (Figure 5-19). At this time, you may meet difficulty if you try to make a major move forward; it may be more advantageous to wait for opportunities to arise naturally, develop from earlier efforts, or come from other people, rather than relying on your own immediate effort and initiative.

2. When the position your year number occupies in the square for a year or month is directly *opposite its home position* in the standard square (Figure 5-20). At this time things may not go as expected, so you'll need some flexibility.

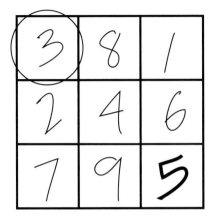
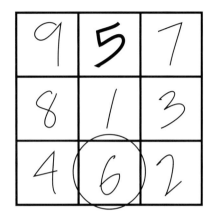

5-19. Examples of numbers occupying positions opposite the number 5.

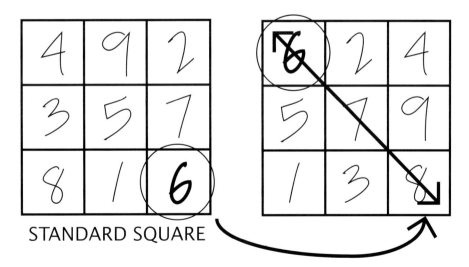

STANDARD SQUARE

5-20. Example of a number occupying the position opposite to its home position in the standard square.

3. When your year number is *in the center* of the square for the year or month—that is, in the house of 5. At this time it's again advantageous to let things come to you rather than go out looking for them.

If you understand these influences correctly, you can see them as yet another way of working creatively with the prevailing energy rather than feeling frustrated by it; the time will come when you're in the right position for more dynamic steps. If you really want to take dramatic steps at these times, the best strategy may be to allow a partner who is in a more favorable magic square position to take the initiative, while you serve as backup or support to that person. You can also use the mitigating effect of advantageous month positions to reduce the limitations of your year position somewhat. Ultimately, though, it's always wise to do whatever the time is best for, and make the most of it. Each stage plays a creative and meaningful role in the whole cycle.

THE EFFECTS OF THE SEASONS

Let's look at another way to work effectively with energies that change over time—by taking into account the interaction of the seasons with your astrological makeup. Seasonal energies primarily affect you through the elements at work at a given time rather than through your particular year number. There are two strategies you can use to work with them.

The first strategy is to use your understanding of the Five Elements to get the most out of the seasons to which they belong. Pursue activities that are appropriate for that element and take advantage of the kind of energy that is prevailing. Traditional societies have always followed these patterns, with great benefit. Here's a brief summary; you'll find a fuller description in Chapter 2.

WINTER: Water element; good for inner development and quiet preparation for later action

SPRING: Wood element; good for beginning projects and raising enthusiasm

SUMMER: Fire element; good for activities that require short bursts of energy rather than sustained commitment

LATE SUMMER: Earth element; good for settling down and becoming more focused

AUTUMN: Metal element; good for reaping the benefits of earlier efforts and for sustained concentration such as study

Even if you live in a climate where the seasons are not so distinct, these influences still prevail at the corresponding time of year, because the atmospheric energies are controlled by these elements.

The second strategy is to use your understanding of the elements to make the most of your native season, the one that corresponds to your element, as shown in Figure 5-21. You will tend to feel at home or in your element in the season corresponding to the element of your year number. For instance, if your year number is one of the earth types, the late summer season may be when you are at your most creative, and you should make sure that you make the most of this. Likewise, on a smaller scale, the late afternoon hours may be your most productive hours.

THE TIME OF DAY

Just as there is a major cycle of changing influences over the years, and a shorter cycle of more superficial change from month to month, there are also changing influences over the course of the day. Observing this pattern can be very helpful in planning your daily activities. It can also make itself felt in terms of health, energy, and well-being.

Each number has a particular time of day when its element prevails, and so this is its "home" position—the time when people with that number are in their element.

ELEMENT	TIME OF DAY	SEASON
FIRE (9)	MIDDAY	SUMMER
EARTH (2, 5, 8)	AFTERNOON	LATE SUMMER
METAL (6, 7)	EVENING	FALL
WATER (1)	NIGHT	WINTER
WOOD (3, 4)	MORNING	SPRING

5-21. The numbers and their corresponding elements, times of day, and seasons.

For some elements, this happens during the middle of the night. Figure 5-21 shows the elements and numbers with their corresponding periods in the 24-hour day. The times of day belonging to elements aren't affected by time zones; they depend on the movement of the sun wherever you are.

The time period when you're in your element may well be your most creative period, when you can generally get more done in a given time. Wood people—3s and 4s—will probably have the highest energy in the mornings. Earth people—2s, 5s, and 8s—may well get their best ideas in late afternoon. Water people—1s—are in their element until dawn, but this doesn't mean they should override normal human biorhythms and stay up all night. It simply means that water energy is most prevalent at this time, and they'll be more themselves.

Whatever your number or element, you can make use of the element potential that goes with the different hours of the day. For instance, if you want to do some communication or PR work, the fire hours around noon will generally be favorable—especially good for a lunch meeting, as long as it's early. The night, of course, is generally best for "water" activities—resting, recovering reserves, being quiet—but with the potential for inner development and letting the unconscious work through sleep and dreams. Going clubbing all night clearly works against this natural rhythm. You can draw many more such useful conclusions for yourself by looking back at Chapter 2 for insight into which elements support which kinds of activity.

TAKING THE LONG VIEW

You'll get much better results from your planning—and feel more fulfilled along the way—if you adopt a holistic approach to harmonizing your decision making with your position in the houses. In other words, don't just look at the present time and try to achieve everything right now; take a longer term view. Consider blocks of time together—sequences of months and especially years. Use the phase you're in to its best advantage and make the most of your potential within it; then do the same with the next phase. Don't take steps now that would be better taken later. This way, you'll create a cumulative effect that will make those steps more successful when you get to them.

If you're thinking of taking a really major step like launching a new business, for instance, and you're in the 1 house for the year, you would do best to use that year for very early planning. The following year, in the house of 2, you'll be well placed for making preliminary arrangements. The year after that, when you're in the house of 3, will be far better for the actual launch, with the following year serving to further build up your new business. At the same time, though, you'll also need to take into account the three "year-square" situations when extra care is called for, mentioned above on pages 114–116.

If you simply can't wait—for example, if you're years away from an auspicious house but you need to move forward with a business plan or other life decision soon— you can always use the cycle of monthly houses in the same way. For instance, you can choose the best month for new projects, decisive action, or having a needed rest. Alternatively, you can have other people who are astrologically better positioned carry out key activities for you.

A Tool Kit for Life

You're now in possession of an incredibly powerful tool for increasing your happiness, fulfillment, and success. You now know how to draw on more of your own personal resources, how to make the very best of a relationship, and how to make the most of the potential that arises over the months and years. Let's now look at a few further guidelines for making the best use of the information you have at your fingertips.

USE WHAT YOU KNOW

The best approach is to become familiar with the underlying principles of sudoku astrology—the nature and patterns of the influencing energies—rather than using the information from the tables, diagrams, and descriptions inflexibly and without understanding or only knowing about your own number. This way, you will get a more profound grasp of the system. You will gain deeper insights. You will be able to adapt the principles to the kaleidoscopic variety of individuals and situations you meet. You will be able to figure out what's going on when something doesn't quite seem to follow the predicted pattern. Remember, the indications here are general tendencies and underlying patterns rather than fixed rules with fixed results; when they operate in life, there are always many other factors at work. We are all unique—all 6,709,711,246 of us (at press time) on this planet.

If you become familiar with all the number types and their qualities, not just those that figure in your own personal chart, this will also pay off. Not only will you understand people around you better, but you will have a much deeper grasp of the nature of the nine houses that you are perpetually passing through, which are so closely related to the nine types of personality energy.

Remember, too, that life never stands still. You can increase your understanding of how you are, and how a situation is, at any moment, but the forces acting upon you are never static. So you'll need to appraise things afresh constantly, not only to understand what is happening, but to adapt to it and harmonize with it, in order to live your life to the best of your ability. Standing still means losing out.

More important still, remember that nothing is predetermined. It's a mistake to think that the indications or predictions from any astrological system—ancient or modern, Eastern or Western, however sophisticated or highly developed—are carved in stone. We interact with the energies of the cosmos using our own creativity, instinct, judgment, and free will. Nevertheless, you can probably manifest your greatest potential *only* if you also take into account the forces and natural laws at work in the universe around you. This timeless system of knowledge and philosophy is one of the most practical ways to tune in to these cosmic patterns.

Yet the astrological aspect is still only half of any situation; the other factor is what you do about the situation once you've obtained your insights. Let's look at relationships, for instance. No partnership will run smoothly on favorable astrological factors alone. No matter how much you know about the machinery of your relationship—no matter how good your "owner's manual" is—you still have to get the thing to work. So it still comes down to the same familiar ingredients for relationship success—commitment, respect, trust, communication, give-and-take, and all the rest. The difference is that astrology can help you solve the thorniest question of all—which of these you need most, and when!

POINTERS FOR SUCCESS

The best way to use astrology is to put it into practice in a holistic way. In other words, don't look at astrological indications, such as what to do and when to do it, in isolation: put them in the context of the rest of your life. If you're figuring out how to make better decisions, have better relationships, be more successful, or enjoy life more, this means integrating the suggestions that arise from astrological analysis with other criteria. Here are some pointers that may help.

1. Don't focus too much on the concept of being "lucky" and using astrology to bring more luck into your life. Life doesn't randomly happen to you— it's very much in your power to influence your experience. Use astrology to highlight possibilities and challenges, and then find ways to transcend any limitations you become aware of. For example, instead of trying to win the lottery on "auspicious" days, why not take practical action to improve your financial circumstances? Make a plan to cut back on spending, or pursue an activity that generates income. You can still use insights from sudoku astrology to get the best results from these more realistic and dependable steps.

2. Have an attitude of self-determination rather than being subject to the idea of an inviolable preordained destiny. Likewise, don't feel that your fate is sealed by what other people do. People who complain about life are giving their power away; people who do something about it are taking that power back.

3. Develop a holistic view of what you want from life. Don't focus too narrowly on particular things you want and particular problems you wish would go away. Instead, see these desires or challenges in terms of the bigger picture and set goals in those terms. You'll find some examples of this approach in the pointers that follow.

4. Be prepared to change in order to achieve results. As the saying goes, "If you keep on doing what you're doing, you'll keep on getting what you're getting." Everything is cause and effect. If you make causes, you'll get effects. If they're good causes, they'll be good effects.

5. Nonetheless, bad things sometimes happen to good people. Life inevitably delivers things that we'd rather it didn't—even when we use astrology wisely! That's part of the human condition. Rather than hoping for a life without difficulties, seek to regard these challenges as opportunities to grow by overcoming them. The way we human beings are designed, this process is actually an essential step on the path to happiness. Without it, we wouldn't be able to develop the wisdom and courage or the skills we need for life.

6. Make sure you include in your life a chance to do the things you love doing. Astrology can help by pointing you in certain directions, but the key indicator is your own passion and sense of joy. Don't risk ending up lying on your deathbed thinking, "I wish I'd built my own house in the woods," or "I was so sure I had an epic novel inside me," or "If only I'd found time to do more macramé." By all means use sudoku astrology to learn more about your own particular qualities and strengths—but then make sure you find your dream and follow it.

7. Living in the present moment is extremely empowering. It's essential to plan for the future and review the past, but dwelling on a past you can't change or fretting excessively about a future you can't control drains your power. The present moment is the point of power; it's the only time when you can actu-

ally do anything. Realize that you can be happy now, rather than putting it off until some time in the future when certain conditions are met—when you've found the partner of your dreams, or when your worst problem has gone away, or when you've magically become very very rich.

8. Cultivate a positive outlook on life. People who expect the worst are rarely disappointed. No, that's not quite right: they get what they expected but are still disappointed! Much better to go through life giving yourself the best possible chance to attract good experiences. Gratitude is the key factor here—the opposite of complaining. People who cultivate the habit of being grateful have a better time. It's even possible to be grateful on occasion for an experience you'd rather not have had in the first place.

9. Think of the universe as a place of abundance rather than scarcity. This is entirely in keeping with sudoku astrology's essential principles, grounded in the Oriental view of a universe full of creative energy, ready to be manifested. Astrology can help you manifest it, but your own attitude is crucial in getting the best results.

10. Don't focus entirely on your own well-being and the things you need for yourself. Just about every religion or spiritual method acknowledges that considering the needs of others around you is crucial to your own deeper happiness and fulfillment. Sudoku astrology can help you find ways to treat others better by understanding the energies that influence them, but you need the motivation too.

11. Try to communicate positively. The things you say, and the way you say them, not only express what's going on inside you but also influence you very strongly. How you describe your own circumstances to others is a good example: it really affects how you feel about those circumstances, and what you can do about them. For example, how do you respond when someone

asks how you are? Do you always find something to grumble about, or do you prefer to look for something positive to report? And when difficulties arise, do you tell people "This sort of thing always happens to me," or is it more like "Something challenging is happening and I'm determined to turn it around"?

12. Activate your own personal energy and healthful vitality by being active, eating well, getting enough rest, connecting with the natural world, and enjoying the changing seasons. This will also enhance your self-awareness and sensitivity to the changing energies around you, helping you make better decisions and get better results from your application of sudoku astrology principles.

13. It's probably worth saying again: Don't let judgments arising from astrology overcome your common sense. Astrology always involves a degree of generalization, and you're a totally unique individual—with your own free will.

TUNING IN TO LIFE

Finally, develop your own instinct about what's best for you, and learn to trust it. As you gain experience and become more familiar with how the subtle and intricate pattern of energies and influences works, you will find that applying it becomes second nature to you. You will notice yourself guessing people's numbers before knowing their birth date; you'll know you're in a certain astrological house before checking the tables. This is when it gets really interesting, really rewarding, and really effective, for you've now entered the intuitive phase. You're starting to tune in to the energies with the subtle sensitivity that all human beings have, bypassing the conscious mind.

With time and practice, this instinctive ability can be a more powerful resource than your conscious mental faculty, which is all too often clouded by emotion, prejudice, or the wish to believe that what you hope for is true. If you succeed in developing this profound, intuitive connection with the cycle and flow of life's energy, you will discover all the more about your own truest nature and realize all the more of your highest potential. You will truly be in tune with the rhythm of life.

So please use this amazing oracle to reach out for whatever you want in your own life and in your precious connection to other beings: more freedom, perhaps; more ecstasy and less agony; more fulfillment, success, mystery, fun, excitement, intimacy, passion, companionship, or love. Whatever it is, go for it!

Acknowledgments

Thanks to Michio Kushi and Herman Aihara for introducing me to this subject, and to Simon Brown for deepening my understanding. Thanks to Daisaku Ikeda for inspiration.

At Sterling, thanks especially to David Nelson, Kate Zimmermann, and Anne Barthel.

Thanks to my agent Susan Mears, and to Elaine for ongoing support.

Index

Euler, Leonhard, 5

family roles of the nine numbers, 74
finding your numbers, 18–23
fire people (number 9 type): overview, 42–43;
    chart of season, time of day, organ system,
    and food taste, 46
fire stage, 12
fire trigram, 42
Five Elements: analysis of elements in rela-
    tionship, 68–69, 70; basic concept, 10–13;
    compatibility of, 66–67; control cycle, 68,
    69; and correspondences, 46; cycle, 11;
    mediating elements cycle, 83–84; numbers
    associated with each element, 13; origin of,
    6; support cycle; 68–69; supporting
    elements, 67, 84–85
Five-Element control cycle and support cycle,
    67–69. *See also under individual stages:*
    water, wood, fire, earth, metal
Fu Hsi, 7

harmony, 113
harvest trigram, 38
health and physical constitution, 45–47
heaven trigram, 36
house of 1 (water), 100
house of 2 (earth), 101
house of 3 (wood), 102
house of 4 (wood), 103
house of 5 (earth), 104–105
house of 6 (metal), 106
house of 7 (metal), 107
house of 8 (earth), 108

house of 9 (fire), 109–110
houses: calculating which you occupy over
    time, 94–95; effects and use in relationships,
    110–114

I Ching and trigrams, 8, 26, 28, 30, 32, 36, 38,
    40, 42
interpreting numbers of another person, 53
interpreting a sample chart, 44–45

launching a business, 119

magic square: history and origins, 2, 5–7;
    measuring compatibility, 63–64; nine
    squares in cycle, 22; over time, 88–119;
    principles, 5–14; standard square and ele-
    ments, 13
mediating elements in relationships, 82–84
metal people: chart for season, time of day,
    organ system, and food taste, 46; number 6
    type, 36–37, 73, 56–57, 67, 79, 80; number
    7 type, 38–39, 57, 67, 73, 79, 80
metal stage, 12
month numbers: calculating which you are in
    or will be in, 96–97; charts and diagrams,
    51, 96, 97; explanation of, 20; finding,
    20–21, 51; and influences, 91, 94; overview,
    16–17; and personality types, 25; signifi-
    cance of, 53; using, in relationships, 63,
    86–87
mother earth trigram, 28
moving water trigram, 26

nine character types, 15, 53–58, 77–80.

About the Author

Irishman Gerry Maguire Thompson lives in England. Gerry has studied Oriental cosmology since 1979, and he is the author of a number of books on personal development and humor, some of which are listed below. To contact Gerry Thompson, visit www.sudokuastrology.com.

OTHER BOOKS BY GERRY MAGUIRE THOMPSON

The Shiatsu Manual
The Shiatsu Box
Cats Are from Venus, Dogs Are from Mars
Astral Sex to Zen Teabags
Meditation Made Easy
Encyclopedia of the New Age
Atlas of the New Age
Knitting Patterns from Atlantis (a novel)
Feng Shui Astrology for Lovers

Details of these and other books can be found at www.gerrythompson.co.uk.